ESSENTIAL
TOOLS

Equipment and Supplies
for Home Gardeners

Karan Davis Cutler

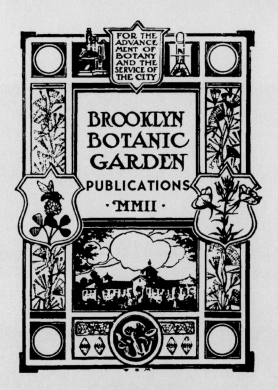

Janet Marinelli
SERIES EDITOR

Sigrun Wolff Saphire
ASSOCIATE EDITOR

Mark Tebbitt
SCIENCE EDITOR

Anne Garland
ART DIRECTOR

Steven Clemants
VICE-PRESIDENT, SCIENCE & PUBLICATIONS

Judith D. Zuk
PRESIDENT

Elizabeth Scholtz
DIRECTOR EMERITUS

Handbook #170
Copyright © 2002 by the Brooklyn Botanic Garden, Inc.
Handbooks in the *21st-Century Gardening Series,* formerly *Plants & Gardens,*
are published quarterly at 1000 Washington Ave., Brooklyn, NY 11225.
Subscription included in Brooklyn Botanic Garden subscriber membership dues ($35.00 per year).
ISBN # 1-889538-50-7
Printed by Science Press, a division of the Mack Printing Group.
Printed on recycled paper.

TABLE OF CONTENTS

INTRODUCTION

CHOOSING THE RIGHT TOOL FOR THE JOB

KARAN DAVIS CUTLER

THERE IS NO RECORD of whether or not an orchard ladder was used to pick the forbidden fruit, but in *Paradise Lost,* John Milton did observe that Eve was not

> … with bow and quiver armed,
> But with such gardening tools as Art, yet rude,
> Guiltless of fire had formed, or Angels brought.

We don't know where Eve shopped, but we do know that stone implements were used two million years ago and that metal tools emerged in the Bronze Age. Exactly when a sharp stick became a dibble or a forked branch evolved into a hoe with a metal head is unrecorded. More complex tools appeared in the 17th century, but the design for nonmechanical garden implements was well set by the time of the Greeks and Romans. Tools that followed have been variations on these basic patterns.

That's not to say that there isn't anything new—or at least different— under the sun in the garden tool, equipment, and supplies department. A quick look at current catalogs turns up products that would not have been found at an agora: a Pine Cone Trapper from a "small shop just outside Sylvester, Georgia" and hinged "pick-up" rakes; Predator Pee ("100 percent fox, coyote, bobcat, and wolf urines") to protect your plants from marauders and the Original Bug Shirt to protect you against biting insects; stained-glass stepping stones and plastic water-lilies designed to sit on plastic lily pads; Victorian-style toad houses and Water Worms that "take the guesswork out of watering."

To be fair, there are garden innovations that are terrific: The floating row

Opposite: Equipment options for home gardeners are enormous. Look for tools that are versatile and sturdy; they will last a lifetime.

A durable, well-made tool, such as the dibble at left, should have a hardwood handle, a high-carbon steel head, and a sturdy connection between the two.

cover is one of the great inventions of the last 50 years. New materials have made products stronger, lighter, and longer-lasting, and ergonomic tools have made gardening easier. If the job is both big and heavy, most gardeners don't complain about gasoline motors, even if they are loud, smelly, and hazardous.

Our equipment options have been enormous ever since the late 19th century, when a single company, such as C.T. Skelton (Sheffield, England), regularly manufactured three dozen different spades, most of which were available in a variety of sizes, weights, and styles. By the early 1900s, thousands of different spades and shovels were available. The trick then, and now—especially for new gardeners—is to choose wisely.

It's so darn easy to get carried away. Everything looks useful. Everything seems necessary. In fact, only a few tools are indispensable; significantly, most of them are versatile. A common garden hoe, for instance, is designed to cultivate the soil and remove weeds, but it can also form rows and furrows, pull soil over seeds, tamp soil, build mounds and beds, create ditches, hill up plants, clobber clods, and dig holes. Mark its handle and it's a yardstick. Swing it wildly and it's a weapon for discouraging the neighbor's cat from using your perennial border as a litter box.

Deciding what to buy isn't your only challenge. You'll also have to choose between models, grades, and sizes of the same tool. But that's good news. If your garden is small and your soil fecund, you don't need an industrial-strength spade. If your back is persnickety, you'll want a long-handled shovel, not a short-handled one. If you're short on heft, choose a 1-gallon watering can, not a 3-gallon model. And don't be put off by terms like "ladies' spade," even if you've sired five sons.

Look for a handle that's not painted, so you can see that the wood is knot-free and runs the length of the handle.

Be Goldilocks: Try several models and sizes, then settle on the tools that are "just right" for you.

You can spend a fortune on garden tools, equipment, and supplies. If you've got a fortune to spend, go to it! But where you live and what kind of gardening you do should also influence what you buy. In cold areas like mine, gardeners swear by cloches and cold frames; in hot regions, shade cloths and irrigation systems are commonplace. City gardeners living tooth-by-jowl with their neighbors may put barrel composters at the top of their list, while country gardeners throw their vegetable waste on a pile and spend their money on electric fences and rototillers. If your garden consists of window boxes or patio pots, you won't need a wheel cultivator, no matter how quaint the ads. Unless it's to serve as an ornament, of course.

SIGNS OF QUALITY

Other than the space you plant, tools and equipment are a home gardener's biggest investment. But you don't have to break the bank, and you don't need every gizmo or gadget that packs store shelves and fills garden-catalog pages. Wise purchases will last a lifetime. Buy the best you can afford.

At the same time, don't be bamboozled by glossy catalogs that sneak a few appallingly expensive imported spades with teak handles in between French rose gauntlets and thatched birdhouses from Devon priced $100 and up. European garden tools are among the best, but exceptional equipment is manufactured in this country too, and is sold at local farm stores and nurseries and at national chain stores (look for brands that come with a lifetime guarantee). Don't forget mail-order companies that specialize in garden tools and equipment for ordinary gardeners not requiring imported marble obelisks and Edwardian hose reels. These firms offer the widest selection of domestic and imported garden tools and equipment (see "Open for Business: Mail-order and Online Sources," page 102).

Prices differ rather shockingly, so compare and shop wisely. For example, the price of a Felco #2 pruner, the most popular model of the most popular pruner, ranges from $33.50 to more than $50. Unless a firm is having a going-out-of-business sale, though, there aren't many "deals" on garden tools. Cut-rate prices usually mean cheaper construction. Before you reach for your wallet or credit card, take a good look at the item's materials and craftsmanship.

HANDLES. Spade, hoe, rake, lopper, whatever, most gardeners should look for handles made of hardwood, such as ash. The grain should be knot-free and run the length of the handle. Softwoods are commonly used in inexpensive tools. Avoid them, and beware of handles that have been painted, a ploy used to disguise softwood.

Tools with steel handles are designed for professionals. They're stronger than wood but more costly, and most home gardeners don't need their extra heft. Fiberglass, solid-core fiberglass, and wood/fiberglass composite handles are light and strong but will boost the cost of a tool by at least one third.

METALS. Today the best garden tools are made of high-carbon steel. Keep your eye out for the words "heat-treated," "forged," "drop-forged," and "tempered." Avoid anything made from "stamped steel," which is less strong. Nor do you want spades, shovels, or forks—tools for big jobs—that are made from aluminum, although aluminum is suitable for trowels and other small hand tools.

Stainless steel tools have great cachet. They don't rust, but they're too expensive for most mortals and no stronger than high-carbon steel. And though stainless steel tools hold an edge better than high-carbon steel tools, they are extremely difficult to sharpen. Don't be tempted.

CONNECTIONS. The soft spot of most garden tools is the connection between handle and head. Cheaper tools come with either open-socket construction (the handle is half-wrapped in a short welded metal collar that's open in the back) or tang-and-ferrule construction (the metal head has a prong, or tang, that is inserted into the handle, and the connection is wrapped with a short metal collar, or ferrule). High-quality tools join handle and head with a solid-socket or solid-strap connection (the handle is inserted in a long metal collar and secured with pins). This method makes tools heavier, but the gain in strength offsets the gain in weight.

MOTOR MATTERS

Gasoline- and electric-powered tools are beyond the scope of this book, but there are two power implements that are indisputable time- and muscle-savers: rototillers and chipper/shredders. You can garden for a lifetime without owning, or even using, either. But if you have illusions—or delusions—of garden grandeur, power equipment offers major-league advantages. Now, however,

Designed to cultivate the soil and remove weeds, a common garden hoe serves many other purposes, such as forming rows, pulling soil over seeds, and hilling up plants.

you're into spending serious money, credit card charges in four figures for large, powerful models, and you're talking noise, air pollution, and motor maintenance.

If your first instinct is, "Don't go there," but you dread hours spent with hand tools, consider renting power equipment. Or organize a group of friends and make a mutual purchase. Cooperative ownership has its pitfalls. Just remember that you invested $250, not $2,500, and be patient when a co-owner forgets to refill the gas tank.

AND SO FORTH

Finally, not all garden equipment has to be relentlessly practical. An item I wouldn't do without is a New England weather stick, a 10-inch debarked branch with a bit of base wood attached, which you nail on a protected outdoor wall. On good days, the branch points up, and in rainy weather it points down. It tells you what you already know. A masterpiece of low technology.

And don't overlook garden ornaments, traditional or whimsical. A sundial, perhaps, or a hummingbird sculpture that moves with the breeze, or a woven bee skep. I have a jaunty wooden sun medallion, made by a Vermont chain-saw artist; and whirligigs, while not especially practical, are colorful and fun. It's *your* garden, so add anything that strikes your fancy. But be careful when shopping for garden ornaments. The English garden writer Beverley Nichols once set out to buy a simple sundial and came home instead with an 18th-century stone balustrade, "60 yards of solid rock." Buyer beware, indeed!

BASIC TOOLS FOR
HOME GARDENERS

KARAN DAVIS CUTLER

ONE OF THE BEST PARTS of any new undertaking is amassing the equipment. Think about what's required to take up bike riding these days. There's the shirt (with logo), the black shorts, the shoes, the gloves, the helmet, and the rain gear—and that's just to outfit *you.* Then there's the $3,500 bicycle and its accessories, the mirror, the saddlebags, the rack, the drink bottle, the odometer …

Gardening isn't any different. Faced with so much good-looking equipment in stores and catalogs, it's easy to believe that you need it all. So take the advice of a middle-aged gardener who has a shed full of tools that do nothing but take up room. Go slow. Be timid. Start with the basics, the implements for digging, cultivating, raking, and carrying. Two years from now the dandelion digger with "magic fingers" that looked indispensable in the store will be gathering dust while your shovel will be bright from constant use.

In fact, it takes only a few tools to make a small garden, so don't skimp on quality. Buy the best you can afford. By "the best" I don't mean a $180 English spade manufactured by a company with an appointment to Her Majesty the Queen. But do purchase well-made tools and equipment that will be worth passing down to grandchildren years after you've sown your last seed, or your last wild oat, whichever comes later. Labels like "professional grade," "nursery grade," and "construction grade" typically mean "better grade," so watch for them.

DIGGING

Digging is usually the gardener's maiden voyage, and a digging tool should probably be your first purchase. There are three basic choices—shovel, spade, and garden fork—and you can start with just one. But realize now that before long you'll want one of each.

Each of these three is made with either a long handle or a short handle ending in a YD- or T-shaped grip. Long handles give you more leverage, but they're also easier to break when you try to pry boulders or old Chevy engines

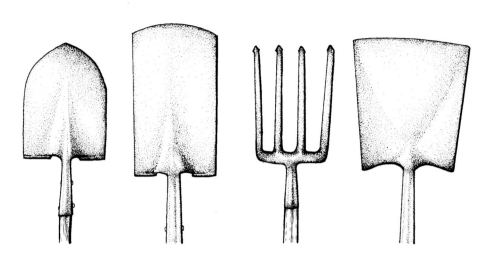

Tools for digging, from left to right: A round-point shovel, spade, and garden fork are essential for garden work. Start with one, but eventually you'll want all three. A square-point shovel is more useful for construction jobs than for gardening.

out of your asparagus bed, and they require more upper body strength. If you choose a short-handled model—my favorite design because it's strong and easier to control—be sure that the top of the handle comes to your waist when the blade is sunk in the ground. Any shorter and you'll need more than a shower after a morning in the garden. (For the record, a folk remedy for lower back pain is a hot poultice of birch leaves, bark, and catkins.)

Whether shovel, spade, or fork, it should have a flat lip, or tread, on the top of the blade to protect your feet. Tool heads should be made from 14- or 15-gauge tempered high-carbon steel, *not* stainless steel, and the blade should be attached to the handle with a solid-socket or solid-strap connection. A hardwood handle is fine—don't spend extra on fiberglass or steel unless you're double-digging eight hours a day (see "Introduction: Choosing the Right Tool for the Job," page 4, for the basics of tool quality).

SHOVELS. A shovel, which has a slightly concave blade with a rounded bottom edge, or point, is *the* American digging tool, and it would be my first choice. The blade, or head, of a shovel is attached to the handle at a slight angle, a design for digging as well as turning, scooping, and moving soil, sand, gravel, compost, and other materials without destroying your back.

There's an array of head sizes and shapes, but the standard is the *common*, or *round-point, shovel*, which weighs between 5 and 6 pounds; its head measures about 8×12 inches. If a shovel feels too heavy or large—remember you have to lift what the head holds—choose a smaller version. The head of a *floral shovel* is smaller, about 7×9½ inches, and is easier to maneuver in close quarters yet plenty big enough for general garden work. Smaller still is a *border shovel*, its 6×8-inch head perfect for digging small transplant holes. *Square-point shovels* (a flat-bottomed model intended for shoveling loose materials, not digging) and *trenching* and *drain shovels* (with long, narrow heads designed for ditching) are made primarily for construction jobs, not for gardening. $35 to $75.

SPADES. The *garden spade* is the classic English digging tool (the name comes from *spada*, Latin for "blade"). It has a nearly flat, rectangular blade, a straight or very slightly curved bottom edge, and a short handle capped with a YD- or T-shaped grip. It's terrific for digging, removing sod, cutting through roots, edging, and trenching. It's less good for turning soil or scooping. Standard spades weigh 5 to 6 pounds and have blades that measure about 7×11 inches.

There are also spades with narrow blades for trenching and ones with smaller heads (5½×9 inches) for small hands and muscles that are known as *ladies'* and *border spades*. Whatever the size, be sure yours is made of heavy, tempered steel, has treads to protect your feet, and has a hardwood handle at least 28 inches long that's connected to the blade with a solid-strap joint. And keep it sharp. $45 to $75.

FORKS. *Garden*, or *spading, forks*, which are spades with tines rather than a blade, are made for turning and aerating the soil and for digging perennials and root crops—not for making holes. Despite their limitations, I wouldn't be without one. Nearly all garden forks are short-handled (about 30 inches with a YD grip), have four 10- to 12-inch flat tines, and weigh about 5 pounds.

Look for a fork with a head no wider than 7 or 8 inches—wider models are awkward to control—and stay away from the *English pattern fork*, which has square tines and usually is lead-heavy, or from forks with round or slimmed-down tines. Tines are easily bent, so the fork head should be made of heavy-gauge tempered steel. *Border forks* are downsized garden forks, good for smaller gardeners and smaller jobs. The *broadfork*, which has two handles attached to a foot bar fitted with tines, is a tool guaranteed to do nothing but rust in your tool shed. *Bedding* and *manure forks* belong in the barn or in paintings by Grant Wood. $35 to $65.

RAKING

Like Rodney Dangerfield, rakes don't get much respect. Almost no one puts them on her or his favorite-tools list, yet every experienced gardener has one and uses it often. It is the tool par excellence for breaking small clods and smoothing the soil, for drawing up and mounding soil, for leveling beds and borders, for pulling out stones and odd bits of debris, for spreading compost and other soil amendments, for covering seedbeds. Enough said.

A *garden rake* is not the same as a lawn, or tine, rake—that tool you reluctantly pull out when the maple leaves have blanketed the lawn. There are two garden rakes to choose between, bowhead and flathead. A *bowhead rake*, my favorite, gets its name from the curved steel rods, or tangs, that run from each end of the head and attach it to the handle. The design creates a little "give"

Opposite: Beautiful and useful, a bamboo lawn, or tine, rake comes in handy in fall when leaves have blanketed the lawn.

Mounding soil, leveling beds, and pulling out stones are some of the jobs for a garden rake. The head of a flathead rake connects flush with the handle, forming a T.

when you use the rake. The head of a *flathead rake* connects flush with the handle, forming a T.

All bowhead rakes have curved teeth; flatheads come with either curved or straight teeth. Look for models that have teeth spaced about an inch apart and a head between 14 and 16 inches wide. Anything wider is difficult to control and may be too heavy to use for more than 15 minutes. And make sure that your rake head is made from a *single* piece of tempered, high-carbon steel—no welding—and has a hardwood handle. $30 to $45.

You won't be happy if you choose a *grading*, or *contractor's, rake*, which looks like a very wide flathead garden rake, or if you are seduced by a light-weight aluminum model. Ditto a *thatching rake*, which resembles a garden rake but is intended for the lawn. And don't forget the most important thing about a garden rake: When you lay it down, make sure the teeth are pointed toward the ground. Trust me on this one.

CULTIVATING

It seems as if every garden season brings a new hoe, and if not a new design, a new twist on an old design. And why not? Few tools are as versatile as a hoe, and most gardeners spend more time with a hoe than with any other tool. Which hoes—notice the plural—you buy should depend on you and your garden. Rather push a tool than draw it toward yourself? Do you plant vegetables in wide, straight rows or is your garden a tightly planted perennial bed? Answer

A bowhead rake gets its name from the curved steel rods that run from each end of the head and attach to the handle. The design creates a little "give."

those questions and then make your choices, remembering that there is no one hoe that is exactly right for every cultivating job. Press me, though, and my first choice would be a common hoe, then an oscillating hoe, and in third place, a tined hoe.

COMMON, OR GARDEN, HOE. This is the hoe you'll find most often in garden centers and other retail stores. It has a broad, flat head, or blade—about 6×4 inches—sharpened on the outside edge, weighs between 2 and 3 pounds, and has a long handle (anywhere from 50 to 70 inches) attached to the head at a 70- to 90-degree angle. It's also known as a *pattern hoe* and as a *draw hoe*, the latter name coming from the way you draw it toward yourself when you use it.

Cheap models are sold everywhere, so be sure that yours has a head and neck that are not welded but made from a single piece of forged steel. The head should be attached to the handle with a socket secured by rivets, and the handle needs to be long enough so that you don't have to bend way over when you work. Expect to pay at least $25. Some models, known as *swan-* or *gooseneck hoes*, have a long, curved shank, or neck, that joins the blade and the handle. I think a gooseneck is hard to manage, but many gardeners swear by them.

A pint-sized version of the garden hoe is the *floral hoe*. This cut-down version is too light to be of much use—recommended only if you're 10 years old or weigh less than 75 pounds. Another common hoe variation is the *onion*, or *Southern, hoe*, which has a long, narrow head (7×3 inches) and is made for shallow weeding and cultivating. Similar is the *collinear hoe*, designed to be

15

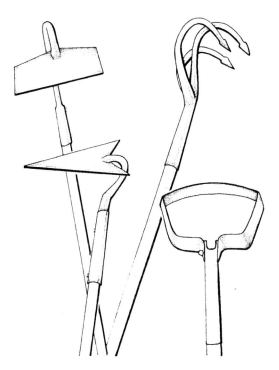

Tools for cultivating, clockwise from top left: common hoe, tined hoe, oscillating hoe, and Warren hoe. Which ones you choose will depend on your style of gardening.

used with your thumbs pointing up. Its head measures about 6×1 inches, and many gardeners find it too light and difficult to control.

The common hoe and its look-alikes are all close descendents of the paterfamilias of the category, the *eye*, or *pattern, hoe*. The first name comes from the blade, which has an oval "eye" (like the hole in an ax head) through which the thick handle fits. It's a tool for tough jobs—it's also known as a *grub hoe*—and has a large head, about 8×7 inches, a relatively short handle, and weighs about 6 pounds. It's overkill in most gardens, a killer for most gardeners. $25 to $50.

WARREN HOE. An American original, first sold in the 1870s, the Warren hoe is shaped like an arrowhead, point down. The head, which measures about 4×6 inches, has no cutting edge but is good in close quarters and for creating holes, upending weeds, and making and covering furrows. $25 to $35.

OSCILLATING HOE. The oscillating hoe, also known as the *action hoe, stirrup hoe,* and *hula hoe*, has a stirrup-shaped head that is hinged to its handle. The head is sharpened on both sides, so you both pull and push it along the ground. It's ideal for cutting weeds just below the soil's surface, but it is not designed for digging, grading, chopping, or cultivating. Make sure yours is made of tempered steel. $20 to $30.

A variation on this theme, another weeder, is the *scuffle*, or *Dutch, hoe*, an unhinged version with various head shapes—triangular is most common—that normally are sharpened only on the front edge and cut on the push stroke. $30 to $40. Another type, the *circle hoe,* made *Sunset Magazine*'s list of the 100 best inventions of the 20th century, but it doesn't make mine. It has a circular head, as the name implies, which gives you only a tiny cutting surface. $25.

TINED HOE. This is a great, light tool for uprooting small weeds once your garden is planted and for aerating the soil around new and established plants. Its head, which should be forged and not welded to the neck, or tang, consists of four slightly curved tines. $30. (There are one-tine models called *finger hoes,* which you do *not* want to buy because they are useless.) For really heavy work, consider a *hook cultivator.* It's almost identical to a tined hoe but tough enough to have pleased Goliath. $35 to $45.

CARRYING

There's always something in the garden that needs to be somewhere it isn't: a load of compost, a clump of daylilies, four flats of annual flower seedlings, two dozen tomato stakes, 5 cubic feet of mulch, and more. You'll want a vehicle for carrying big loads. Forget about the purple, fat-wheeled, molded-plastic yard buggy that looks as if it belongs on the moon and choose between a two-wheeled garden cart and a wheelbarrow.

GARDEN CARTS. Garden carts are three-sided boxes mounted on two bicycle wheels. They're large enough to hold several bales of hay, strong enough to handle loads of 400 pounds, yet easy to push (or pull) and to balance. Get one that is made of heavy plywood and has inflatable tires and a hinged panel in front (for easy dumping). And buy the large model (between 3 and 4 feet wide): If you do enough hauling to need a garden cart, you need the big one. $175 to $300.

WHEELBARROWS. A wheelbarrow is a tray with two handles and a wheel underneath. In some form, it's been around for about 2,000 years, which ought to be recommendation enough for any gardener. It's less stable than a cart—you have to balance it when moving—but it can go up and down narrow rows and turn on a dime.

Increasingly popular, garden carts are easier to maneuver than wheelbarrows, yet able to handle bulky or heavy loads.

Don't waste your money on an inexpensive, lightweight "lawn" wheelbarrow. Instead, look for a model with an extra-deep tray, called a *contractor's wheelbarrow*. Be certain yours has an inflatable wheel at least 4 inches wide (for stability) and a seamless tray if it's made from steel (heavy polyethylene trays, which are both light and rustproof, are an excellent alternative to steel). $100 to $175.

For a small or patio garden, a *bucket* may be all you need for toting things to and fro. If you can't pick up a free 5-gallon plastic bucket at a construction site, buy a galvanized steel model. Or consider one of the new *collapsible weeding buckets* made of strong, vinyl-coated polyester, for hauling the spoils of an hour spent weeding. $33 for the 30-gallon version, $22 for the 10-gallon model. Mine keeps me from being a garden Gretel, always leaving a trail of debris and hand tools.

A *trug*—a shallow, oblong basket made of strips of wood—is the traditional English mode of transporting cut flowers and herbs. In addition to being useful, a trug will make you look picturesque as you snip thyme, bay, and parsley for a bouquet garni. $40 to $125. To pick flowers in style, consider a *galvanized French floral bucket,* $25 to $30 for an extra-large model (18 inches tall), $18 to $20 for a 12-inch medium one. *Wire-mesh baskets* are meant for carrying the bounty of your vegetable patch. They're strong but open, so air can reach the produce, and you can hose them and their contents down before you go indoors. $15 to $25.

Finally, *tarps and plastic sheeting*—or old sheets and bedspreads—are great for moving the weeds you've pulled, the leaves you've raked, and the clippings you've cut to the compost pile.

The short-handled bulb planter makes a neat transplant hole for the nasturtium being installed amid some strawberry plants.

HAND TOOLS

Although anything without a motor qualifies as a "hand tool," most gardeners have short-handled implements in mind when they use this term. How and where you garden dictates how often you'll need hand tools. If you're a down-on-your-knees, nose-in-the-dirt gardener, or if your growing takes place on a patio or deck, hand tools are for you. Garden Tools of Maine is one name to look for if you want strong, durable tools.

Trowels are the backbone of this family of implements, often sold as part of a three-tool set: trowel, fork, and claw. The others are occasionally useful; the trowel is a must.

You'll need a trowel for digging modest holes in prepared soil and working in containers of all kinds. Wide-blade models are better for garden chores, *narrow-blade,* or *transplanting, trowels* are for excavating in pots, tubs, barrels, and boxes. You'll find an array of cheap trowels made from stamped metal for sale, so be careful when you buy. Pick a one-piece metal trowel, either aluminum or stainless steel, or a trowel with a tempered carbon-steel blade connected to an ash handle by a solid socket. A good trowel costs $12 to $18.

If trowels are the hand-tool equivalent of spades and shovels, *hand forks* are the scaled-down version of garden forks. Most have three sturdy tines, and like their big brothers and sisters, are designed for cultivating the soil. *Claws,* which look like a three-fingered, half-open hand, are also made for cultivating and weeding. $12 to $18.

You may also find heavy-duty versions of this hand-tool trinity, most with handles 15 inches long and heads mounted at right angles to the handle by an eye socket. It's an ancient design, suited for vigorous work and vigorous workers. Contemporary ads contend they "eliminate kneeling." Unless you can touch your toes and hold that position for ten minutes, don't believe it.

I'm enthusiastic about my *hand cultivator,* a Korean tool with a short wood handle and a curved, carbon steel head that resembles the blade of a plow. I use it to loosen soil, make and cover furrows, dig holes, hill up plants, and uproot weeds. $13 to $18. It may appear in stores and catalogs as an *EZ-Digger* and a *hand plow.* Pass on the long-handled version.

Tools for weeding, from left to right: Cape Cod weeder, dandelion weeder, and weeding knife. Hand weeders are especially useful in a garden that is too tightly planted for a hoe to be safely used.

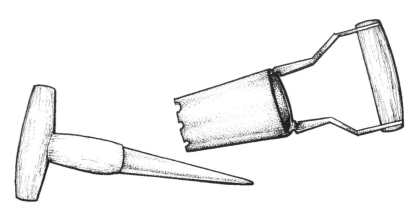

Tools for planting: dibble, left, and bulb planter. Use a dibble to poke a hole in the soil for seeds, bulbs, and transplants. A short-handled bulb planter works best in prepared soil.

You may want to take a close look at *hand weeders*, especially if your garden is too tightly planted to use a hoe safely. The *Cape Cod weeder* is a New England favorite. Shaped like the letter L and made in Maine by Snow & Nealley, its narrow blade is meant for cutting weeds just below the soil's surface. About $18 for the 9-inch-handle model. *Dandelion,* or *taproot, weeders* are designed for getting out weeds that have taproots. Most have a long, narrow blade with a forked tip. $8 to $10. If you're a patio gardener, consider a *patio knife,* a tool for weeding between bricks and stones. $10.

The Japanese use *a weeding knife,* which has a 6-inch blade that is sharpened on both edges (one smooth, one serrated); it's also known as a *soil knife* and *farmer's weeder* and can be used for any cutting job. $15. And if you come across a *Jekyll weeder,* which looks like a tuning fork with a wood handle and was a favorite of the British garden maven Gertrude Jekyll, give it a try. Better still, send it to me—I've been looking for one for years.

Two hand tools are especially useful for planting: a *bulb planter,* which is an open-ended cone sharpened on its bottom edge, and a *dibble.* A short-handled bulb planter doesn't have the oomph to pierce turf but is great for making planting holes in prepared soil. $5 to $10. (For naturalizing bulbs in turf, buy a heavy-duty bulb planter with a long handle and a foot tread, $45.) A dibble, or *dibber,* is an evolved stick—use it to poke a hole in the ground for seeds, bulbs, and transplants. Truth be told, you can use a sturdy stick or a broken hoe handle. But a dibble is an essential tool just because it's so beautiful. You need one, if only to look at.

ET CETERA

What tools and equipment come next? You'll eventually need a file, of course. Paying good money for a top-notch shovel or hoe is a waste unless you have a file to keep it sharp. When the time comes, look for a *bastard file.* The term refers to the file's teeth and has nothing to do with its family history. Pick one that is at least 10 inches long, either a flat mill file or a half-round model, which is flat on one side and half-round on the other. $10 to $15.

And before long, you'll need a *soil thermometer.* At planting time, the temperature of the soil is as important as the temperature of the air. A good one costs about $30, a cheap model about half that. While you're browsing the "measurements" section of the garden catalog, buy a *rain gauge* ($5 to $10) and a *maximum/minimum thermometer* ($25).

The list could go on and on. The authors—experts all—of the chapters that follow will guide you through the "material world" of other, more specialized garden activities. Their recommendations are worth following. But begin with a few of the basic tools described above. And wait on everything else until *you* need it.

PAINLESS GARDENING

Now that I'm on a first-name basis with osteoarthritis, I have a new interest in tools made to reduce stress and strain on the body. Every year there is more "enabling equipment" to choose from, not just ergonomically designed tools and other useful items, such as kneelers and wheeled seats, but adaptive devices for standard tools. There are special handles to attach to hoes and rakes, extensions for short-handled tools, padded grips, and more. Manufacturer names to look for are Earth Bud-Eze, Sure Grip, Fist-Grip, and E-Z; Fiskars also makes a line of ergonomic hand and cutting tools.

Ergonomically designed tools, such as the enabling trowel above, as well as adaptive devices for regular tools, reduce stress and strain on the body.

FEED ME!

SUPPLIES FOR ENRICHING THE SOIL

JAKE CHAPLINE

"I T'S EASY TO MAKE AN IMPRESSION on a soft head," my grandmother used to say, usually with a glance in my direction. I guess that explains why I always think about *The Little Shop of Horrors* when I'm working in the garden in the spring. In the 1986 film—the musical version—Seymour, the klutzy owner of a flower shop, harbors a carnivorous plant from outer space in his greenhouse. Whenever he goes into the greenhouse, the plant demands, "Feed me, feed me." At first, when it's small enough to be satisfied with a few drops of blood, it has a chirpy little voice, but by the time it's large enough to start preying on the neighbors, its voice is a rolling basso profundo.

So there I am in the garden in May, swatting blackflies and setting out seedlings and hearing in my mind a chorus of little voices saying, "Feed me." I give the transplants a good dose of manure tea—the first of several they'll get over the next few weeks—to encourage them to stretch their roots into the garden soil, where they will find everything they need to feed themselves. Manure tea is where I draw the line—no chemical fertilizers, no fresh blood, no neighbors.

Seymour should have heeded the organic grower's adage: Feed the soil, not the plant. It's sound advice, even if you're sure your zucchini won't turn on you. Why? Because it's easier to feed the soil with organic fertilizers than it is to feed the plant with synthetic chemicals.

Let's digress for a moment to try to clarify the distinction between "organic" and "chemical" fertilizers. Manufacturers of synthetic fertilizers like to point out that *all* fertilizers are chemicals, regardless of their source, which is perfectly true. It's also true that some synthetic fertilizers are organic in the chemical sense; that is, they are carbon compounds. So it's easy to be misleading, accidentally or intentionally, in using these terms to label fertilizers.

Originally, "organic fertilizer" was a term applied only to materials that came from living (or once-living) organisms: mulches, manures, blood meal,

Collect yard waste and kitchen scraps and turn them into compost. Use the nutrient-rich black gold to fertilize garden plants, such as the hosta above.

bonemeal, and so on. But some soils require amendments that aren't found in sufficient quantities in animal and plant materials—certain minerals, for example. So organic farmers and gardeners turned to natural, although not necessarily organic, sources for these amendments, such as powdered rock. Over time, the meaning of "organic fertilizer" expanded to encompass a variety of naturally produced, minimally processed materials.

Chemical fertilizers are generally synthesized from inorganic chemical compounds, such as ammonium sulfate for nitrogen, superphosphate for phosphorus, and sulfate of potash for potassium. Fertilizer manufacturers argue that plants don't care where their nutrients come from and that chemical fertilizers supply them more efficiently. The problem is, chemical fertilizers provide only the nutrients that the manufacturers put into them, and only for a short time. Because they are water-soluble, chemical fertilizers are available to plants as soon as they are applied. They produce results more quickly than organic fertilizers, but they also leach away quickly. You have to be careful with them, applying just the right amount of the right nutrients at the right time. Too much can hurt the plants, and if the chemicals are applied too early or too late, the nutrients won't be available when the plants need them.

You don't have to be nearly as precise when using organic fertilizers like compost, well-rotted manure, and cover crops (green manures). They release nutrients more gradually while adding humus to the soil, improving its texture and feeding bacteria, earthworms, and other beneficial organisms. Humus-rich soil holds soluble nutrients like a sponge, so they don't quickly leach away. Over time, the soil in a well-tended organic garden keeps getting richer, making more and more nutrients available to plants whenever they need them.

ESSENTIAL NUTRIENTS

Sixteen elements are known to be necessary for plant growth. Air and water supply three of them: carbon, hydrogen, and oxygen. The rest are taken from the soil. Only three of these—nitrogen, phosphorus, and potassium—are used in such large amounts that they must be replaced routinely to keep the soil productive. The others—calcium, magnesium, sulfur, boron, copper, iron, manganese, molybdenum, zinc, and chlorine—are required in relatively small amounts and are unlikely to become depleted.

Nitrogen, phosphorus, and potassium are the N, P, and K listed on the labels of all-purpose fertilizers. The numbers on the labels—5–10–5 or 10–10–10, for example—indicate the percentage of N, P, and K (always listed in that order) by weight in the fertilizer.

There are a number of readily available sources for all of the nutrients needed by plants (see the chart on the facing page). You'll find some of them right at home—in your kitchen waste, grass clippings, and leaves. Others, like

Rock phosphate, made from powdered rock, is a natural source of phosphorus. A naturally produced, minimally processed material, it is considered an organic fertilizer.

APPROXIMATE NUTRIENT VALUES
OF VARIOUS FERTILIZERS

Organic Fertilizers	Nutrients N–P–K	Additional Nutrients and Comments
Alfalfa meal	5–1–2	
Blood meal	15–2–1	
Bonemeal, steamed	2–11–0	
Chicken manure, fresh	1–0.9–0.5	
Cocoa shells	2.5–1.5–2.5	
Coffee grounds, dried	2–0.4–0.7	
Colloidal phosphate	0–25–0	Also supplies calcium
Compost	NPK varies	Good source of micronutrients
Cottonseed meal	6–2–1	
Cow manure, fresh	0.5–0.2–0.5	
Dolomite (dolomitic limestone)		Raises pH, source of calcium and magnesium
Eggshells	1.2–0.4–0.1	Source of calcium
Epsom salts (magnesium sulfate)		Source of magnesium and sulfur
Fish emulsion	5–2–2	
Fish meal	10–4–0	
Granite dust	0–0–5	Source of trace minerals
Grass clippings, fresh	0.5–0.2–0.5	
Greensand	0–1–7	Source of magnesium and trace minerals
Gypsum (calcium sulfate)		Source of calcium and sulfur
Horse manure, fresh	0.6–0.3–0.5	
Kelp meal/liquid seaweed	1–1–3	Good source of micronutrients
Limestone		Raises pH, source of calcium
Peat moss		Lowers pH
Pine needles	0.5–0.1–0	
Rock phosphate	0–30–0	
Seaweed, dried	1.5–1–5	
Seaweed, fresh	0.4–0–0	
Soybean meal	7–1–2	
Straw	0.6–0.2–1	
Sulfur		Lowers pH, necessary nutrient
Wood ash	0–2–7	Raises pH

In the continuous composter on the left, a compost pile is built gradually. The batch composter on the right is filled all at once. Rotate the barrel to keep the compost aerated.

livestock manure, might be had free for the asking if there are farms in your area. Many organic fertilizers and soil conditioners can be found at good garden centers or in garden-supply catalogs.

Even if the soil in your garden has all the necessary nutrients, plants may not be able to make use of them. The nutrients are available only if the soil is at the right pH level. The pH scale measures the acidity or alkalinity of the soil, running from 0 at the acid extreme to 14 at the alkaline extreme. A pH of 7.0 is neutral. The scale represents a geometric progression, so pH 5 is 10 times as acidic as pH 6 and 100 times as acidic as pH 7. Most vegetables and flowers like slightly acidic soil with a pH of about 6.5.

It's easy to test your soil's pH with an inexpensive kit or with a more costly pH meter ($50.00 and up), either of which you can pick up at a garden center or purchase by mail. If you'd like a more extensive test done by experts, you can send a soil sample to the agricultural experiment station at your state university, where it will be analyzed for a fee. (Many private labs provide the same service.) A standard analysis—$12 at my state university—checks the pH, soil texture, and major nutrients. For a little more money, you can have the organic content tested and determine the soil's texture class, based on proportions of sand, silt, and clay.

Since acids are produced by the decay of organic matter, garden soils tend to become increasingly acidic as compost and other organic materials are worked in. You can counter this by spreading finely ground limestone on the garden in the fall, using a broadcast spreader. Depending on how heavy the soil is, the addition of 50 to 80 pounds of limestone per 1,000 square feet will raise the pH by one point.

If you are starting a garden with soil that is too alkaline, you can lower the

Commercial bins are space-saving but not essential. In most situations a simple compost heap will work fine. You can also build your own two- or three-bin system.

pH gradually by digging in organic matter. Adding sulfur compounds, such as aluminum sulfate or copper sulfate, will lower the pH faster if the soil is much too alkaline.

BEAUTIFUL COMPOST

Sometimes it's difficult to tell if a person is primarily a gardener or a composter. Not so with my father, who is clearly a composter. He has kept a compost pile perking in the far corner of his backyard since 1954, when he and my mother bought their house. Now 80, he still delights in finding special things to add to the pile—a pickup load of sawdust and horse manure from the fairgrounds, a bucket of rotten apples from a nearby orchard, a few bales of spoiled hay, leaves collected from the neighbors. Given his choice, I suspect he'd have himself added to the pile when the time comes.

It's easy to understand that kind of devotion. Composting is a form of alchemy, changing garbage into nutrient-rich black gold. And while some people follow precise formulas and procedures in building and tending their compost piles, it's really a simple process. Basically, you collect a heap of organic stuff and let it rot. It will do that on its own, but there are some steps you can take to speed up the process and improve the result.

The principal alchemical agents in a compost pile are bacteria, and they need four things to work their magic: air, moisture, carbon, and nitrogen. They work best when the ratio of carbon to nitrogen in the composting material is about 30 to 1 (see "Food for the Compost Bin," page 29). Many things you might want to add to your pile—straw, sawdust, pine needles, and autumn leaves, for example—have too little nitrogen to decompose quickly, so they

27

should be mixed with matter that is relatively rich in nitrogen, such as manure, kitchen scraps, and leguminous plants. The rule of thumb is that nitrogen-rich material should make up about one fourth of the volume of the pile. You can also increase the ratio of nitrogen by sprinkling a little bonemeal, blood meal, or cottonseed meal on top of any material you add to the pile.

One way to mix the compost components more thoroughly and to give the composting process a head start is to shred high-carbon materials like leaves before adding them to the pile. Power shredders are specifically designed for this purpose, and they'll even chew up small branches. They are expensive, however—$500 or $600 at the low end. I find that a lawnmower with a mulching blade does a satisfactory job on leaves. I just rake them into windrows 3 or 4 inches high and run over them a few times. Another option is to fill a garbage can half full with leaves and use a string trimmer to chop them.

Many garden stores and catalogs offer a product called compost starter or activator—Super Hot is one brand. It's supposed to jump-start the composting process, but you don't need it. If you build up your compost pile in layers, with a few inches of rich garden soil between each layer, the soil will provide all the activator you need.

A compost pile can be just that: a pile of vegetative stuff in an out-of-the-way corner of the yard. But it looks better and is easier to manage if it is confined to a bin of some sort. I have made bins out of wooden pallets, using one as the bottom and standing four on end and wired together at the corners. I have also made them out of wire fencing, rolled into a vertical cylinder and supported by metal fence posts. Both types worked fine, except that the wire-cylinder arrangement was awkward when I wanted to turn the pile. It's better to have a

Opposite: Build a compost
pile and worms will come.
In northern climates, where
compost piles shut down over
the winter, you can continue
composting throughout the
year with an indoor worm bin.

FOOD FOR THE COMPOST BIN

Materials	Approximate Carbon–Nitrogen Ratio
Nitrogen-rich Materials	
Chicken manure, fresh	10:1
Coffee grounds	20:1
Cow manure, fresh	20:1
Fruit waste	20:1
Grass clippings, fresh	17:1
Hay	15:1
Horse manure, fresh	25:1
Pig manure, fresh	10:1
Rabbit manure, fresh	8:1
Seaweed	17:1
Sheep manure, fresh	15:1
Vegetable waste	15:1
Weeds, fresh	20:1
Carbon-rich Materials	
Animal manure with bedding	45:1
Corn cobs	150:1
Corn stalks, dry	60:1
Leaves, dry	60:1
Newsprint	400:1
Sawdust	300:1
Shrub trimmings	50:1
Straw	80:1
Wood chips, hardwood	500:1
Wood chips, softwood	600:1

bin with one side that can be opened. Any kind of enclosure will work, as long as air can circulate through it and water can drain out.

Or you can buy one of the ready-made compost containers that come in various designs and sizes, ranging in price from less than $20 to more than $200. Most are made of recycled plastic, and many have lids—a particular advantage if you are an urban gardener and have to do your composting right under the eyes and noses of your neighbors.

There are two types of prefab containers to choose from. Continuous composters are basic outdoor bins in which you build a compost pile gradually. Batch composters, with capacities ranging between 7 and 12 cubic feet, are filled all at once. Barrel-like batch composters are sometimes called tumblers, because they are mounted in a frame you can rotate to turn the compost and keep it aerated. They make compost very quickly—in as little as three or four weeks, according to advertising claims—but you'll need another container to hold the refuse for the next batch. Unless you are in a real hurry for finished compost, you'll probably find a continuous composter more convenient.

Give the composting process a head start: Use a lawnmower with a mulching blade to shred leaves, which are high in carbon, before adding them to the compost pile.

In northern climates, outdoor compost piles shut down over the winter, when it becomes too cold for the bacteria and other decay agents to keep the process going. But you can keep composting throughout the year with an indoor composter that uses redworms to digest vegetable scraps and convert them into nutrient-rich castings (both compost bins and worms are available from mail-order firms). Worm composters can work well, but you have to be careful to keep the compost mix balanced. If the amount of compost overwhelms the worms or the moisture level is too high, the contents of the composter can turn into a slimy mess.

Other products developed for compost enthusiasts include aerators, which are tools for poking holes in the pile, and soil thermometers that let you monitor just how well the pile is heating up. Each of these items costs about $20. They might be useful if you are really determined to compost as efficiently as possible, but they aren't necessary. You will, however, need a bucket with an airtight lid to collect vegetable waste in the kitchen and a good spading fork for turning the pile.

In the summer, the composting process in an ordinary outdoor bin takes about three months, although it can go much faster if the pile is built in layers and tended carefully. It should be turned every few weeks, or whenever you notice that it is shrinking. Many gardeners build side-by-side compost bins, moving the compost from one bin into the other.

GREEN MANURE AND MULCHES

Another good source of humus is green manure—a cover crop that is turned under before it has a chance to flower. Reserve a portion of your garden for cover crops and rotate them to a different section each year. You can also grow cover crops in garden paths to prevent soil compaction, keeping them mowed for a neat and trim look. Or you can sow them in beds from which early-maturing vegetables have already been harvested.

There are many good cover crops to choose from. Most are planted in the spring and turned under in the fall, while they are still green and succulent. Some, such as sweet clover, rape, and certain varieties of vetch, are biennial. They will not flower the first year, so they can be planted in the spring, left in the ground over the winter, and then turned under the following spring, after new growth appears. Winter rye and field bromegrass are two hardy crops that are often planted in the fall for winter cover and then turned under in spring.

Cover crops not only add humus to the soil, they also develop extensive root systems that keep the soil loose and collect nutrients. Legumes, including clover, vetch, soybeans, and cowpeas, make particularly good fertilizer because they collect free nitrogen from the air, store it, and slowly release it into the soil after they are turned under. Seeds for common cover crops are sold at garden centers; for a better selection, you'll want to shop by mail.

Mulching the garden is another way to add organic matter to the soil. Many gardeners use straw, leaves, and other organic materials to prevent weeds from sprouting in paths and around plants that require lots of room. Some leave the mulch in place permanently, adding to it year by year. The underlayers gradually decompose, fertilizing the garden from the top down—a system modeled on nature's own. Other gardeners turn the mulch into the soil at the end of the season.

PLANT BOOSTERS

Even if you have built up the soil in your garden, your plants will benefit from an extra shot of fertilizer from time to time. You can provide this with synthetic products such as Miracle-Gro and Rapid-Gro, with side-dressings of manure or compost, or by watering with solutions of fish emulsion, seaweed emulsion, or manure tea. Since I have ready access to horse manure from a nearby stable, I use manure tea. I make it by putting a couple of pounds of manure in a 5-gallon bucket, filling the bucket with water, and letting it steep for a day or two before using it to water my plants.

I use manure tea on transplants when I set them out and give a weekly shot to flowering and fruiting plants when they begin to set buds and to vining plants as soon as the vines start to run. Probably the plants would do fine without this extra fertilizer, but they need watering anyway, and the fertilizer lets them know I care. After all, if there are any talking plants out there, I want them to be saying nice things about me.

EQUIPMENT FOR WATERING THE GARDEN

CHARLES W.G. SMITH

WATERING IS A TASK most of us gardeners must do again and again, and any repeated chore can become tiring and tedious, robbing us of the pleasures of gardening. Poor watering tools are not worth the price exacted from body and soul. Fortunately a number of high-quality tools exist that make watering easier and more enjoyable.

WATERING CANS

Watering cans have been used to irrigate plants for centuries. The anatomy of a watering can is simple: a cylinder-shaped reservoir, a handle, a spill shield to prevent water from overflowing, and a spout topped by a rose to deliver water in a gentle spray. Over the years, these basic parts have been redesigned and recombined to produce an amazing array of tools. Though some watering cans are poorly designed, badly made, and a waste of your money, many others are functional works of art.

A basic decision comes early: metal or polyethylene? Poly is cheaper, lighter, and doesn't rust or corrode. Metal is better looking. Companies including Haws and Dramm offer high-quality cans in both materials. Buy a model that you can get under your faucet and that you can carry comfortably when full.

HAWS CAN. In 1886, Englishman John Haws designed a watering can that has been the standard of excellence ever since. The Haws can is artistic, functional, and well balanced. The extra-long spout delivers the water where the water is needed, and the innovative bunker-shaped spill shield prevents water from slopping out of the can. Another feature of most Haws cans is the rose: typically oval in shape, it is turned up so the water falls ever so gently on plants and soil.

Genuine Haws watering cans, made in England but sold throughout the

The Haws can has an extra-long spout that delivers water exactly where it is needed, and the bunker-shaped spill shield prevents water from slopping out of the can. It is designed so water falls gently on plants and soil.

world, come in a wide selection of styles, sizes, materials, and finishes, with most plastic models priced under $30; metal cans run $40 to $90, depending on size. There are many makers of watering cans, but if I were to be offered my choice of all watering cans in the world, I would pick a Haws. They're that good.

TRADITIONAL WATERING CANS. Traditional watering cans are the most common type and also the most frustrating. The reservoir is often too large, making a filled can excessively heavy; the spill shield is frequently ineffective; the spout is too short, forcing the handler to tip the can into uncomfortable positions; and the can is unbalanced when full, making it difficult to carry and use. The traditional watering can is inexpensive, which probably accounts for its popularity, but it is not a tool for the serious gardener.

FRENCH WATERING CANS. The classic French can looks like a hybrid between a traditional can and the Haws type. The reservoir is barrel shaped with an often inadequate spill shield at the top; the spout is long and tapered. French cans are an improvement over traditional types but inferior to Haws cans.

CONTAINER, OR CONSERVATORY, WATERING CANS. The container can is designed to deliver water efficiently to plants growing in pots. It has a small

reservoir (2 to 3 quarts) and sports a down-turned spout. Container cans are often designed in the Haws style. Polyethylene cans cost about $15, 3-quart metal models from Haws are $75.

SEEDLING WATERING CANS. Seedling cans are designed to water newly sown seeds, emerging seedlings, or recently transplanted plugs. They look like stubby Haws watering cans and deliver a gentle spray from a cone-shaped rose. Seedling cans are not always easy to find but are excellent additions to the tool-shed of gardeners who do a lot of sowing and transplanting. Top-of-the-line metal cans run $40.

WATERING-CAN ROSES. A watering-can rose is a round or oval tool that directs the flow of water from the can through a screen, breaking the stream into a soft flow. Though roses and water breakers do the same job, rose refers to a tool attached to a watering can, while a water breaker designates the device attached to a wand or hose.

High-quality watering-can roses have a fine-mesh screen that filters the water before it reaches the patterned breaker, preventing the holes in the rose from clogging. The best roses are made of brass. $15.

WANDS

A watering wand is a rigid metal or plastic tube that attaches to the end of the hose and extends the gardener's reach. The best wands are made of metal with a hard plastic or foam handgrip. A plastic or brass shutoff attaches to the base of the wand and a water breaker screws to the top. Many companies manufacture watering wands, but the premier wands are made by Dramm. Its products

Tools for watering, from left to right: Haws can, French can, and traditional watering can. Choose a model that you can get under your faucet and carry comfortably when full.

are well designed, functional, and elegant; lightweight, yet able to take bumps and bangs. Other manufacturers of quality wands are Haws, L.R. Nelson, and Gardena.

CLASSIC WANDS. This aluminum or chrome-plated watering wand used by most commercial growers is 30 inches long and straight with a slight bend near the end. Commonly sold as a set with a shutoff and a 400-hole breaker, a classic wand can be used for just about any type of watering, from irrigating wide rows to soaking hanging baskets. It isn't perfect—it's awkward to use in tight quarters—but it is an excellent all-around watering tool. Gilmour makes a neat telescoping wand that reaches from 30 to 48 inches. Wand sets run between $15 and $40.

PATIO WANDS. Patio wands are about 16 inches long; their compact design makes them easy to handle in tight quarters. Patio wands have either the same or a slightly exaggerated degree of bend at the tip as classic wands and are partnered with a trigger-style shutoff for easy operation and a 170-hole breaker that allows more efficient watering of container plants. Sets are often priced under $20.

HANGING-BASKET WANDS. A hanging-basket wand is similar to the classic wand in design and dimensions with one defining difference: The top bends about 90 degrees. The sharp bend and long reach of this wand allow its 170-hole breaker to reach directly into the container without the user having to resort to gymnastics. $20 to $40.

SPECIALTY WANDS. Some companies offer interesting variations on the traditional wand-and-breaker combination. One, the *watering lance*, is a brass wand with an upturned rose coupled to a trigger or ball-valve shutoff control. It produces a gentle spray, turning a garden hose into a watering can. Haws

makes some of the best watering lances; its 24-inch straight-trigger model costs $85.

Another tool that turns the hose into a watering can is called the *Flower-Shower,* made by Gardena. This lightweight plastic tool attaches to the hose like a watering wand. Dramm also offers some neat specialty products. One is its brightly colored, 16-inch-long wand that comes with a foam handgrip, an oversized plastic shutoff, and a 400-hole breaker ($14). These are made for kids, but I swear by the purple one.

WATER BREAKERS

A water breaker forces the stream of water passing through a wand or hose through a screen, breaking the stream into a soft-patterned flow. As mentioned earlier, water breakers and roses do the same job—a rose is the tool that's attached to a watering can, and a water breaker is the device that's attached to a wand or hose. Most breakers are classified by the number of holes in the screen. As with wands, the water breakers used by many professionals are produced by Dramm. I've used Dramm water breakers for decades. They are close to indestructible yet still affordable.

STANDARD BREAKERS. A 1000 water breaker has 1,000 holes in the screen and breaks the water stream into a very gentle spray suitable for use on delicate plants, seedlings, or newly planted plugs ($10 to $20). A 400 water breaker has 400 holes and is used for general garden watering. (It's also not bad for washing the car.) Plastic models are about $5, aluminum or brass ones cost around $10.

Opposite: Nozzles can be adjusted to produce a range of sprays, from a stinging stream to a drizzly mist. Right: Watering-can roses break the water into a gentle spray.

For watering containers, choose a 170 water breaker. About half the size of a 400 breaker, it produces a narrow stream ($5 to $10).

FAN BREAKERS. A fan breaker produces a wide spray pattern and is designed for watering a large area, such as a seedbed. One warning: It is easy to under-water with a fan breaker because it disperses the water over such a wide area.

MIST BREAKERS. Mist breakers, or *mist nozzles,* are small, round breakers with three nut-shaped openings. They break the water into a fine fog and are excellent for use in propagation. Mist breakers are labeled according to the number of gallons of water that pass through the device in 1 minute. (For example, a breaker rated at 1 gallon per minute would be labeled 1 gpm.)

HOSES

A garden hose is a hollow, flexible tube through which water passes. For a tool so simple, there is an astonishing number of choices. Most hoses are constructed of three or more layers of reinforced vinyl or reinforced tire cord, sometimes with a rubber exterior. The greatest source of aggravation with hoses is their tendency to kink, twist, and turn stiff after time outdoors. Inexpensive hoses are especially prone to these defects.

A soaker hose allows a slow, steady flow of water to escape along the entire length of the hose. It is made of a single layer of porous rubber, and the water "sweats" into the soil.

Rubber is less likely to kink than polyethylene, but it's also heavier. Lugging hoses around the yard is hard work, so don't buy something you can't manage. Whatever material you choose, make sure that any garden hose for use in the yard has a diameter of at least ⅝ inch and that its psi, or pounds-per-inch, burst-pressure rating is 500. Self-coiling hoses (see below), which are intended primarily for watering container plants, are the exception to this recommendation.

BASIC HOSES. A good garden hose should have machined brass couplings, not plastic, built-in washers, a minimum of 4-ply construction, and an exterior that is treated to withstand sun, heat, and cold. I've used many hoses that promised not to kink or twist, and they all ended up kinked and twisted. Except one: The Flexogen 6-ply ⅝-inch garden hose, manufactured by Gilmour, is a gardener's dream. The interior is reinforced with two layers of radial tire cord; the polished exterior resists abrasion; it has a burst rating of 500 psi; it's light; and it has a lifetime guarantee. All this for around $45 for 100 feet.

SPECIALTY HOSES. Some hoses are engineered to perform a specific watering task. Two examples are *soaker hoses* and *drip-irrigation hoses,* both of which save water and time. A soaker hose is a porous hose that allows a slow, steady flow of water to escape along the entire length of the hose. The hose is made of a single layer of rubber, and the water "sweats" into the soil. Most gardeners lay soaker hoses on the soil surface, or you can bury them a few inches beneath the soil or mulch to create a semipermanent and inexpensive drip-irrigation system.

Lay soaker hoses or drip-irrigation hoses on the soil surface or bury them a few inches below the surface to create a semipermanent and inexpensive irrigation system that saves water and time.

Drip-irrigation hoses are usually rather stiff polyethylene hoses pierced with small holes that allow a slow stream of water to bleed into the soil. Simple systems are inexpensive ($35 to $50 for 100 feet) and easy to install, but when you add filters, emitters, pressure regulators, magnetizers, and computer-controlled timers, things get complicated and costly. The bible on the subject is Robert Kourik's *Drip Irrigation for Every Landscape and All Climates* (1993).

If you're a patio or deck gardener, consider a *self-coiling polyurethane hose*. It resembles a long coiled phone cord, like those that were popular before cordless phones became standard fare. They come in ¼- or ⅜-inch diameters, with a 125 psi, and are light and easy to handle. 30 feet of ¼-inch-diameter hose runs about $50; the same length of ⅜-inch hose will cost about $20 more.

TIMERS. Timers are affixed to the water spigot and hose and set to water the garden at a designated time, for a designated duration. Models range from the ingeniously simple and cheap to the complex and costly. The simple models—priced $25 to $30—turn the water on for a set amount of time, then shut it off. More costly models ($50 and up) have touch pads that allow you to program watering cycles days ahead of time. Gilmour and L.R. Nelson offer a good selection of quality models.

NOZZLES. Nozzles are roses with an attitude. Instead of breaking the water into a gentle spray, nozzles can be adjusted to produce a range of sprays, from a stinging stream to a drizzly mist. Although more versatile than roses, nozzles have a history of growing leaky with time; newer models are more reliable, but many poorly manufactured types are still around. You can choose between two designs: straight or pistol grip.

Straight nozzles look like small versions of the nozzles attached to fire-fighting hoses. The water flow through these nozzles is adjusted by twisting the body of the tool; no breaker is required. Be sure to purchase a model made of brass. *Pistol-grip nozzles* consist of a handgrip and trigger combined with a water breaker. They're comfortable to use and often offer a range of spray patterns that can be selected by twisting the water breaker. Prices range between $8 and $25.

ON/OFF VALVES. This simple ball valve is attached between the end of the hose and the nozzle and lets you turn the water on or off. It's a great time-saver, eliminating a trip back to the faucet when you want to change or remove a nozzle. You'll want several—plastic models are about $3, brass ones $15.

SPRINKLERS

Sprinklers are automated watering cans. They water large areas easily and come in an array of styles designed for specific watering tasks. Although sprinklers are time-savers, they also waste water. If you decide you need one, Gilmour, L.R. Nelson, and Gardena are names to look for.

OSCILLATING SPRINKLERS. Oscillating sprinklers swing like a pendulum, sweeping back and forth and spreading water over a rectangular pattern (which can be adjusted). These sprinklers are easy to set up and move. Meant for watering large areas, they vary in price and quality; expect to spend about $40. Both Gilmour and L.R. Nelson offer models with built-in timers.

PULSATING SPRINKLERS. These are the sprinklers you see irrigating cultivated fields, their columns of water shooting out like cannon fire over the crops. Home versions of pulsating, or *impulse, sprinklers* pack a little less punch but are equally efficient at watering large areas. Gilmour makes a large-coverage model with a spray pattern up to 106 feet in diameter, as well as models with timers. Pulsating sprinklers can be set to cover a complete circle or any part of a circle.

Most are mounted on a small grate that can be placed on the lawn; some have a spike design, the sharp end pushed into the soil to anchor the tool. The *rain tower,* or *tree, sprinkler* is a pulsating sprinkler mounted on a metal tower that can be adjusted to various heights; it's especially useful for watering tall perennials and vegetables. Spike models that throw water up to 85 feet cost about $35; tower models cost twice that amount.

ROTARY AND ROTOR SPRINKLERS. The force of the water entering a rotary sprinkler spins its arms to create a circular watering pattern. Rotary sprinklers are good for watering small areas. A Gilmour model has a telescoping feature that allows the sprinkler to be adjusted from 24 to 40 inches tall so it can grow with the garden. Prices range from $8 to $25.

A sprinkler of similar type, called a *rotor sprinkler,* uses a turbine to throw water incredible distances. A supercharged model made by Gilmour, called the

Connected to the end of the hose, a watering wand extends the gardener's reach. The best wands are made of metal with a hard plastic or foam handgrip. A plastic or brass shutoff attaches to the base of the wand, and a water breaker screws to the top.

turbine rotor sprinkler, produces a coverage pattern of 70 feet in diameter, is very quiet, and throws a remarkably even spray.

TRACTOR SPRINKLERS. Tractor, or *walking, sprinklers* have sprinkler arms mounted on a wheeled chassis: The sprinkler slowly rolls across the grass as it waters. Tractor sprinklers—home models that pull a garden hose up to 200 feet and cost around $125—are considered novelties by some; others think they are wonderful tools. In either case, they are fun to watch. Also fun to watch are *sculpture sprinklers*, which "shower the garden with fascinating water dances." Most are made of copper and cover an area of about 30 feet.

SUPPLIES FOR STARTING SEEDS

PETER LOEWER

AMAZED AT THE PROLIFERATION of electronic equipment aimed at absorbing valuable parts of your day? Wondering if you should invest in a do-it-yourself DNA test to make sure you are you? Shocked by the headlines alerting you to the dangers of genetically engineered seeds? Aren't we all.

With the ever-increasing emphasis on gadgets, you might expect new technology to be sweeping the seed industry. There have been a few changes in equipment over the past few years, but most of what's available to home gardeners is only a modification of traditional supplies. So throw complications to the winds, enter the low-tech world of starting plants from seed, and relax.

CONTAINERS

I know a rock-garden enthusiast who visits a local fast-food joint every morning with her husband and winds up each spring with some 700 Styrofoam coffee cups for starting seed. (Recently, blocks of expanded polystyrene have appeared on the market. They measure about 6×3×2½ inches and have 18 holes that hold cylinders of compressed peat. They can be used again and again by simply replacing the peat cylinders.) But if coffee cups, yogurt containers, or plastic jugs aren't your idea of a successful container, look for any of the following—just remember that any container must have drainage holes.

SPEEDLING TRAYS™. Popular commercial versions of my friend's polystyrene coffee cups, these are reusable celled trays with cells that taper toward the bottom so the seedling and its roots pop out with ease. Trays come in sizes from 338 cells to just 32 cells for large seeds. Prices range between $6 and $10, depending on the number of cells per tray. Replacement inserts are $3. (Heavy plastic trays with either 432 or 192 tapered cells cost about $8.)

PLASTIC POTS AND TRAYS. There are all sorts and sizes of plastic containers—

Opposite: The basic tools for starting plants from seed are rather low-tech: an assortment of pots and a sterile potting mix.

Left: Give plastic tubs, milk cartons, and the like a new lease on life by reusing them as seed-starting containers. Opposite: Soil blockers compress moistened potting mix into perfect blocks, ideal for seed-starting.

from 1 to 4 or more inches across—made for sowing seeds. You can choose small individual pots, open flats, flats that are divided into cells, or plugs (which make transplanting less stressful for the seedlings). Most small plastic pots cost only a few cents each; six-cell containers are usually sold in a sheet of 15 ($2), and the flat to hold them is another $1.50.

Many retailers now offer *APS* (short for Accelerated Propagation System) *kits,* which include a solid-bottom flat, a mesh-bottom flat, a capillary water mat, a cell or plug tray (up to 288 cells), and a clear plastic lid for about $12. All plastic containers can be used season after season, but remember to clean them after every use.

PEAT PELLETS AND CONTAINERS. Peat pellets are made of compressed sphagnum peat that expands when it is wet and is held together by a bit of plastic netting. Most are about 1½ inches in diameter and a little over 2 inches high when they expand. Pellets, which require no additional container, are perfect for planting just one or two seeds, but they retain water astonishingly well, so be careful when you use them. The manufacturers say it isn't necessary, but I remove the netting when I set each seedling in the garden. ($10 for 50 pellets.)

Peat pots are made from sphagnum peat moss and wool fiber. Available in various sizes, both round and square, they must be filled with a planting medium, but when it's time to transplant, plant and pot can go into the garden. Although plant roots can penetrate the pot walls, when I plant them out I

always tear away most of the bottom and some of the sides, just to help the roots along. Fifty square 2-inch pots in a plastic holding tray cost about $7.

FIBER PACKS. These containers usually come as 11×21-inch trays (2½ inches deep), divided into six 5×7-inch or ten 4×5-inch containers that can be separated. They're made of recycled cardboard and when they wear out, you can add them to the compost pile. Cheap (six trays of 5×7-inch containers are $12) and popular.

POTMAKER. Here's a cunning wood device (it looks like a pepper grinder) that turns strips of newspaper into 2½-inch pots perfect for starting seeds and housing young transplants. No glue is needed—just roll paper strips into little paper pots that naturally decompose in the ground. A bargain at $13.

SOIL BLOCKERS. Soil blockers come in three sizes: ½-, 2-, and 4-inch. Made in England from zinc-coated steel, these tools compress moistened potting mix into perfect little blocks. There are even pins available to make perfect openings in the soil blocks for the seeds. The 4-inch model is too large for a home gardener, and the smallest model too small. Pick the 2-inch blocker, $25 to $30. Anyone who has used one swears by it.

GROWING MEDIA

There is one caveat when dealing with seed-starting: Whatever medium you use, make sure it's sterile. That bugaboo called "damping-off," an old term for the fungi-caused destruction of seedlings just when the little stems emerge from the soil, is no laughing matter. The easiest and safest solution is to purchase a *sterile* seed-starting mix. There are dozens of products, all widely available and inexpensive—about $5 for a 9-quart bag—and organic mixes are available, if you prefer. The ingredients vary from one product to another, but most are both soil-

45

less and nutritionless mixes; they primarily contain sphagnum peat moss, perlite, and vermiculite in some combination.

If you'd rather, you can make your own soilless medium. Of the various combinations that I've tried over the years, my favorite seed-starting medium is equal parts milled sphagnum peat moss, perlite, vermiculite, and sand.

SPHAGNUM PEAT MOSS. Sphagnum peat moss consists of partially decayed mosses that come from bogs; it is highly acidic and has a fantastic ability to absorb water, up to 25 times its dry weight. For years I started seeds in peat alone, but this proved to be a liability because peat has no nutrition. All seedlings require fertilizer as soon as their true leaves appear. In order to save time and effort, I now plant my seeds in a soil mix but sprinkle a ½-inch layer of shredded peat moss on top of the mix to discourage damping-off.

PERLITE. Perlite is made from volcanic rock that has been heated and crushed. It's used like sand, but it's too light to be used alone and provides no nutrition.

VERMICULITE. Vermiculite is a lightweight material made from mica heated to 2000°F, which breaks it into very small particles. It retains moisture and doesn't pack down, but has no nutritive value.

SHARP SAND. Sharp sand, or builder's sand, has larger grains than common sand—they're rough, or sharp, to the touch. Don't use ocean sand, which is usually too fine and contains salt.

HEATING DEVICES

Seeds and cuttings sprout best when they have bottom heat. The usual recommended location—the top of the refrigerator—has obvious limitations, and there are two good alternatives. Far and away the easiest solution for providing

Opposite: Seeds and cuttings sprout best when they receive bottom heat. The easiest way to provide warmth is with a heating mat. Right: Indoors, emerging seedlings require supplemental light or they will get leggy.

warmth is a heating, or propagation, mat. It's a flat sheet of heavy rubber (sizes vary, but common measurements are 10×20, 20×20, and 28×20 inches) that produces even heat. You just set your tray of seedlings on top of the mat and plug it in. A 10×20-inch mat runs $30 to $35. (There are slightly more expensive setups that include a wire frame with the self-regulating mat, $80 to $95 for a 17×38-inch frame and mat.)

Waterproof heating cables are less expensive ($20 for 12 feet, $25 for 24 feet) but a bit more trouble. Most come with a built-in thermostat set for about 74°F. (You can buy an additional thermostat if you want to adjust the settings; $45.) The cables come in 6-, 12-, 14-, 36-, and 48-foot lengths. The recommendation is 4 feet of cable for each square foot of space. Cables are normally buried in the planting medium, or you can arrange the cable on a layer of masonite or other insulating material, cover it with a layer of sand, and place your trays and containers on top of the sand.

LIGHTS

Unless you start seeds in a greenhouse or outdoors in a cold frame, you've got to have supplementary light; without it, seedlings become leggy in their search for light. What you purchase depends on how many seeds or cuttings you want to raise. Individual lights are fine for just one or two containers of seeds or cuttings. Clamp-on fixtures with black reflectors and full-spectrum fluorescent bulbs run $25 to $30; replacement bulbs are $8 to $10. More ambitious gardeners can pick up an inexpensive fixture at the local hardware store—the traditional hanging 24-inch "workshop" light—then fit it with a full-spectrum fluorescent tube, for about $10.

Homemade or prefabricated, a cold frame is a great place to sow seeds, especially if you install heater cables and turn it into a hotbed.

Light stands are just what the name suggests: metal stands of various sizes equipped with light fixtures. They are wonderfully convenient but don't come cheap, about $500 for a model 27 inches long, 12 inches wide, and 70 inches tall (with four shelves, four fixtures, and eight bulbs). A tabletop model with one fixture and bulb will cost $150 to $250. If you're serious about raising plants from seed, a light stand is worth thinking about.

Emerging seedlings need at least 16 hours of light a day, so whatever kinds or sizes of artificial lights you use, you'll want to have a timer to control them. Timers that offer several cycles per day run about $15.

COLD FRAMES

A cold frame is not just a place to harden off plants or to overwinter tender species. It's also a great place to sow seeds, especially if you install heater cables and turn it into a hotbed. A homemade cold frame made from four bales of hay and an old window works fine, but if you aren't handy in the woodworking department and want something more permanent and better looking, you're in luck.

Prefabricated cold frames will set you back about $125. That buys you a 2×4-foot (18 inches tall in back, 12 inches in front) redwood frame with an insulated polycarbonate light. For another $45 you get an automatic vent operator—heat powered—that will save you from running in and out several times a day. For big-league growers, there is a lightweight PVC-pipe cold frame—6×8 feet—fitted with translucent corrugated polyethylene glazing guaranteed to keep the soil 10 degrees warmer on sunny days. $185.

EXTRAS

In addition to the standard equipment, it's always a good idea to have plenty of white plastic labels ($3 for fifty 5-inch tags) and waterproof pens ($4). Memories are short, and it's easy to forget exactly what seeds were planted in what container on what day. You'll also want a way to water gently—either get a fine rose for your watering can, or buy a misting nozzle for your hose ($10).

SERENDIPITOUS PROPAGATION TOOLS

I've always loved using a tool for a purpose that wasn't intended, probably a remnant of my '60s "question authority" mentality. I propagate more than 1,000 different plants at my West Virginia nursery each year, and the work gives me dozens of opportunities to "misuse" household items. Such as:

CHUPPA KNIFE. They're well made and never rust. Since they're stainless steel, they don't sharpen well, but they're so cheap I don't mind buying a new one. The serrated model is ideal for dividing large clumps of perennials.

PUMP SPRAY BOTTLE. In a commercial setting, cuttings are placed under a mist system. Create your own with an empty pump spray bottle—just be sure you clean it thoroughly first.

MINI-GREENHOUSE. Tired of misting several times a day? Take a Chuppa knife, slice off the bottom of a 1- or 2-liter soda bottle, and you have a little greenhouse to keep your soon-to-be-rooted cuttings from drying out.

ROOT COMB. My friend Norm Beale devised a little gadget for untangling the roots of potbound seedlings: a 1×6-inch piece of plywood with 25 four-penny finishing nails pounded through it. It works like a comb. And if it isn't fine enough, use a real comb.

KITCHEN DRAWER. Not the kitchen drawer itself, but what's in it: Plastic bags, toothpicks, aluminum foil, and rubber bands are all useful in air layering plants. Slice halfway across the stem and wedge it open with toothpicks; dust the wound with a rooting hormone and take a handful of moist, unmilled sphagnum moss and wrap it around the cut. Wrap a plastic bag around the moss and tie it tightly at the top and bottom with rubber bands. Cover the stem with aluminum foil to keep sunlight from drying it out or heating it up. Depending on the type of plant, you will have a mass of roots in anywhere from three weeks to six months.

Your greatest tool is your imagination. Use it, and you will surprise and delight yourself with what you discover.

—*Barry Glick, Sunshine Farm & Gardens*

PRUNERS, LOPPERS, SAWS, AND THEIR RELATIVES

CHERYL DORSCHNER

TRY TO LIVE UP TO EXPECTATIONS of what a garden should be by planting and tending in a frenzy—perennials, annuals, vegetables, trees, and shrubs. My toolshed is a testimonial to my efforts. Yet my gardening heart is where the lawn and gardens end: My idea of pleasure is cutting trails through our woods to reveal clusters of jack-in-the-pulpit and moss-covered boulders. One of our neighborhood goals is to open up connecting paths through the woods behind our houses so we can visit each other without using the highway. This gardening is done with saws, lop-

Bypass pruners are very popular with North American gardeners. They make clean, even, close cuts and are ideal for living plant material.

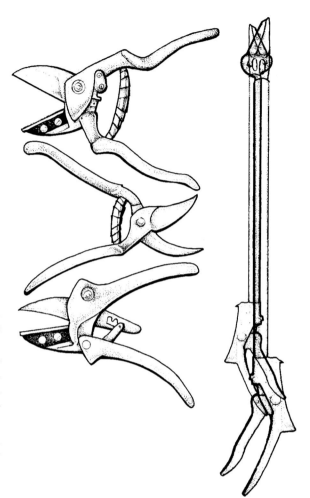

pers, shears, and pruners.

The longer I garden, the more I appreciate well-crafted, durable tools: a pruner whose top handle rises to meet and support the thumb, or a lightweight but sturdy lopper with soft, no-slip grips. Tools like these turn work into pleasure. The wrong trowel will only get the job done awkwardly, but the wrong saw may injure the sawyer and forever damage a tree that's taken 50 years to reach maturity.

Tools for cutting, on the left from top to bottom: anvil pruner, bypass pruner, and pruner with ratchets. Right: long-handled pruner shown at a different scale.

When it comes to settling on cutting tools, try out as many as you can before buying. Don't be shy about asking storeowners to slide a tool out of its packaging so you can get a grip on it. Ask friends if you can try their tools. Take the time to choose the most comfortable tools you can find—ones that feel good in your hands. First and foremost, buy tools that are sized for *you*.

Even the best cutting tools become dull with use, so I look for tools made from tempered steel, which can be sharpened, and for tools for which replacement parts are available. Among the well-known manufacturers of cutting implements are Ames, ARS, Barnel, Corona, Fanno, Felco, Okatsune, and Wallace/Fiskars, but don't feel you must limit yourself to these brand names.

The long handles of loppers allow you to reach places that hand pruners can't, and they provide excellent leverage for nipping larger stems.

PRUNERS

A hand pruner, or *secateur*, is the tool of choice for cutting soft and woody stems up to ½ inch in diameter. It's the tool I use more than any other. To keep track of your pruner, invest in a leather holster for your belt ($12).

Pruners come in two basic styles. *Bypass pruners* have a blade sharpened on the outside edge that slides past a hook; they make clean, even, close cuts. *Anvil pruners* have one sharp blade (sharpened on both edges) that hits a flat surface; they tend to leave a small stub but are unsurpassed for cutting dead-wood. Which is better? "In Europe, the anvil pruner is thought to be better," says Josh Newman, the sales manager for Barnel International, an Oregon tool company. "But North American gardeners feel that the bypass makes a cleaner cut without crushing stems. We sell about 1,000 to 1 bypass to anvil."

The classic bypass pruner is a Felco #2. It's the standard by which others are measured. "They're just plain made of the best-quality materials and crafts-manship," says a representative of OESCO, a Connecticut orchard supply com-pany. Felco #2s have forged steel blades that can be aligned and a shock absorber between the padded alloy handles, and they come with a lifetime guarantee. All the parts of Felco pruners are replaceable. Damage a blade or a spring and you can buy a new one. That's a good deal when the pruners cost between $35 to $65.

Pruners come in left-handed and small-sized models, and with straight, nar-row, and curved blades as well as the standard designs. The Felco #6, for

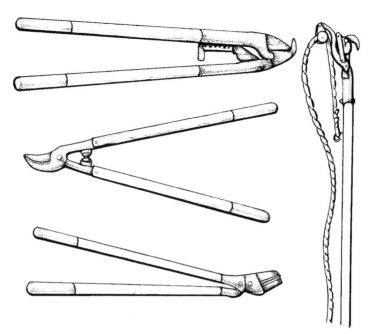

Tools for cutting, on the left from top to bottom: ratchet lopper, bypass lopper, and anvil lopper. Right: pole pruner.

example, is for small hands and small jobs, while the Felco #11 has a narrow, pointed blade for close work. The ARS needle-nose pruner has an even longer blade, designed for cutting the stems of flowers, vegetables, and fruits ($15). Corona is among the firms that makes a bypass cut-and-hold pruner ($40).

Other characteristics fine-tune the differences among pruners. Pruners with ratchets increase hand power a notch at a time, thus allowing you to nip larger stems. *Ratchet tools* are anvil style, and to keep the added ratchet from making the tool too heavy, most are made of die-cast aluminum, plastic, or nylon. Lightweight Florian ratchet pruners cost about $40.

Rolling-handle pruners turn as you grip the handle shut. Originally designed for field-workers whose hands became blistered after long days of pruning, this swiveling action spreads the muscle effort to the entire hand. The results? Reduced fatigue and less chance of tendonitis. Gardeners either love the rolling handle or hate it, so this pruner may not be a good "first purchase." Felco originated the design and sells right- and left-handed models. $50.

One of my favorite pruners, made by Barnel, sports a center bolt with an oil reservoir that self-oils the tool each time you open and close the blade. The company makes a full line of both anvil and bypass pruners, all with the self-oiler. $8 to $26.

Long- or *telescopic-handled pruners* are designed for "out-of-reach" jobs, such as the interior of a shrub rose or a small tree. Most are lightweight, have bypass blades, extensions that range from 2 to 4 feet long, and a scissorlike one-hand grip. Prices for 2-foot models start at $50.

Many pole pruners are fitted with a small saw for removing branches that are too large for the blades.

LOPPERS

While there are both long-handled pruners and mini-loppers, to confuse matters, for the most part loppers are pruners with heavy blades and sturdy handles up to a couple of feet long. They allow gardeners to nab branches in the ½- to 2-inch diameter range.

As with pruners, loppers come in anvil, bypass, and ratcheting (also called "geared" and "compound linkage") styles. Their usefulness is in their handles: They're not just longer, allowing you to reach places hand pruners don't; they also give you terrific leverage. Handles are available in wood, but most gardeners opt for aluminum, tubular steel, or fiberglass with cushioned grips. Choose a lopper that has carbon steel blades and is fitted with "bumpers," rubber cushions that stop the cut when you bring the handles together. Loppers with handles in the 15- to 21-inch range are easiest to work with; heavier and longer-handled models give you better reach and more power. Prices range between $30 and $160 (for the 29-inch ratchet "Power Lopper" made by C.K.).

POLE PRUNERS

Pole pruners, which are essentially pruner blades mounted on the end of a pole, will keep your ladder-climbing to a minimum. You make the cut—up to 2 inches with standard-size models—by pulling on a rope (or sliding collar or lever) that is connected to the blades by a pulley. Prices range from $60 to more than $100.

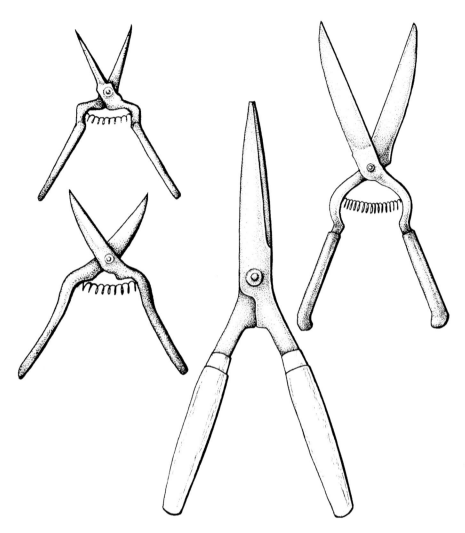

Tools for cutting, from left to right: thinning shears (top), flower shears (bottom), hedge shears, and grass shears. From clipping topiaries to deadheading flowers and trimming grass, shears serve many purposes.

Many pole pruners are also fitted with a small saw for handling branches that are too large for the blades. If you're not trying to reach halfway up a mature maple, Fiskars' 10-foot, rotating-head "Pruning Stik" may be all you need. It's light, yet tough enough to slice through limbs up to 1½ inches in diameter ($75). Corona makes a pruner with a telescoping pole—to 12 feet—that costs $70.

SHEARS

Shears have brought us America's most lamented landscape feature: The "pyramids and meatballs" that mask way too many house foundations. (And the late

20th century compounded the sin by bringing us electric- and gas-powered shears.) But it's not the fault of the tool, and shears are useful in the garden when plants, such as hedges or topiaries, need regular clipping; when flowers, vegetables, and fruits need to be picked; and when herbaceous plants need to be cut back, thinned, or deadheaded. What you buy depends on your garden.

FLOWER SHEARS. Scissors may be a better term for these shears, which are designed for cutting and deadheading flowers. Like scissor blades, both of the slender bypass blades are sharpened; some models are designed to trap and hold the stem when it is cut (Fiskars' version is $20). Heavy-duty models are good for cutting tough fruit stems and small, non-woody branches. $15 to $25.

THINNING SHEARS. Long, narrow blades characterize thinning shears, making them easy to maneuver among delicate plants. Think of them as refined flower shears. $10 to $25.

GRASS SHEARS. Small-scale gardeners who don't want to go electric still get down on their knees and trim grass by hand. Today's models are lightweight and designed with more comfortable grips. $12 to $20.

HEDGE SHEARS. Hedge cutters have long bypass blades, 10 inches long or more, and handles that are about 1 foot long. Shearing a substantial hedge is tiring, so choose shears carefully. Although longer blades cut more per snip, they add weight. Look for shock-absorbing handles and for models designed with wavy blades that cut and hold branches. $25 to $60.

SAWS

When it comes to big jobs, retire your loppers and pruners and get out a saw: For most branches more than 2 inches thick, a saw is required—and not just any saw. Saws designed for garden use are the only ones that don't gum up when you cut green wood.

PRUNING SAWS. A lightweight pruning saw is probably all you'll need. Be absolutely sure that you buy one with a tri-cut blade. (Tri-cut blades are also sold as "turbo-cut," "razor-tooth," "Japanese-tooth," "tri-edged," and "three-sided.") All tri-cut blades cut on the pull stroke. This modern tooth design makes sawing far easier and faster, and cuts so smoothly that the wood feels like it's been sanded. A 3-inch blade is ideal for most work and will cut limbs up to 10 inches.

Tri-cut pruning saws are available with either straight or curved blades. (Curved blades are good for close work and for jobs that are shoulder level or higher.) Tri-cut blades are tricky to sharpen, so pick a model with replaceable blades and one that has a cushioned handle. Prices run $30 to $65. Pruning saws with traditional blades are much cheaper, but don't be tempted.

For small jobs, there are tri-cut pruning saws that fold like a pocket knife. A 7-inch blade is a practical size, easy to carry in a deep pocket. $25.

COARSE-TOOTH SAWS. If you have many big sawing jobs, you may need a coarse-tooth saw, something that will slice through branches and trunks up to 18 inches. These saws come with D-handles and blades between 20 and 26 inches long. (Models with the teeth pointing forward cut on the push stroke;

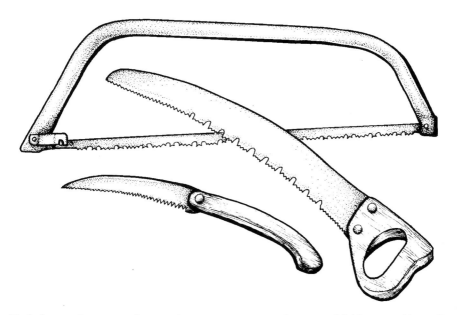

Tools for cutting, top to bottom: bow saw, coarse-tooth saw, and folding saw. You will need a saw for most branches greater than 2 inches in diameter. Saws designed for garden use are the only ones that don't gum up when you cut green wood.

saws with the teeth pointing backward cut as you pull.) If you need a saw this big, look for one with a tri-cut blade. Corona's 21-inch model is $55.

BOW SAWS. The bow saw is the choice of many new gardeners. Its replaceable blade in a C-shaped frame seems like a logical choice, and it's cheap ($15). But it's a tool for the woodpile, not the landscape.

POLE SAWS. The name gives it away: a saw mounted on the top of a pole. It's not an essential tool but occasionally a useful one when you don't want to climb a ladder (and if you pick a tri-cut blade, a *very* useful one). Large blades get very expensive, but a 13-inch saw with grip (you supply the pole) is about $45.

KNIVES

Many gardeners swear by the clean cut of a sharp pruning knife, but I'll never forget the owner of a small seed company who sliced into a 'Purple Marker' potato—and into his own hand. He showed more color than he intended. Pruning knives are dangerous and have little advantage over good pruning shears. For other knife-cutting jobs, a good-quality pocketknife with a carbon steel blade will do.

One category of cutting tools beyond the scope of this chapter is power tools. String trimmers, electric- and gas-powered shears, and chain saws are becoming lighter and more convenient. They have their place—whether it's at your place is up to you.

EQUIPMENT FOR THE WATER ENTHUSIAST

KATHLEEN FISHER

OKAY, HOLD UP YOUR HANDS. How many people have a dream landscape that *doesn't* include water, whether it's an ocean, lake, burbling stream, or Olympic-size gunite pool with multiple fountains? Our instinctive attraction to water explains the growing popularity of water gardening. But building a pool or pond or even installing a half-barrel on the patio scares off many of us who are horticulturally inclined. We prefer to deal with dirt and plants instead of the pumps and filters that go hand in hand with water gardening. Don't despair! A pond need be only as mechanically daunting as you want to make it.

The absolute requirements for a water feature are a container of some kind, from a small basin for the patio to a football-field swatch of liner, and a pump to aerate your water to keep it from stagnating. From there, it's your own choice whether to add flourishes and geegaws, including multi-tiered fountains and colored lighting reminiscent of the Ice Capades.

PREFORMED SHELLS AND FLEXIBLE LINERS

Assuming that you want a full-fledged pond of small to medium size, there are two popular choices: a flexible liner or a preformed shell. If you want a raised or semiraised pond, a heavy shell is your best choice, since it only needs a bit of support around the sides. You *can* use a liner for a raised pond, but you'll need to build a rock-solid support for it.

Preformed shells are made of either semirigid or rigid materials and will cost more than a flexible liner for the same size pond. Depending on shape, prices average about $250 for a 65-gallon model, $1,000 for a 500-gallon shell.

Opposite: Whether you'd like a splooshy sound or crashing drama from your waterfall will determine how powerful a pump you need to install.

Flexible liners offer unlimited possibilities for pond size and shape. Available in stock sizes, liner sheets can be joined to make the perfect pond.

The cost may be prohibitive if you want a very large pool, but preformed shells are a good choice for the design-phobic, since sizes and styles are set.

Liners, in contrast, offer almost unlimited possibilities for shape and size. Although they come in stock sizes, you or your supplier can join the edges of the sheets to make a pond as immense or convoluted in shape as your imagination warrants. Getting liners to your garden site is a snap, since they roll up and fit in a car trunk. A liner may not be the best choice where punctures can be a problem—on rocky terrain or where large dogs with proportionately prominent nails roam. And a liner won't last as long as a shell.

Liners aren't sold under brand names but by the material from which they're made and by thickness. You'll find books that talk about butyl liners, but these are rarely available in the United States. Suppliers in this country offer EPDM (ethylene propylene diene monomer) or PVC (polyvinyl chloride) liners. *One warning:* EPDM, a synthetic rubber, is also used for roofing products, in which case it can contain toxins that kill fish and plants. *Never* use roofing materials as liners for your water garden.

EPDM liners range in thickness from 30 to 45 mil (a mil is one thousandth of an inch). Because they're resistant to ultraviolet light, they will last from 20 to 30 years, longer than PVC liners, and they're stretchier than PVC liners, making it easier to lay out irregular shapes. They're also more expensive, running about $350 for a 20×20-foot sheet. The most commonly available PVC ranges from 20 mil, which will last from five to seven years, to 32 mil, which will last 10 to 15 years. A 20×20-foot PVC liner will cost you about $250.

An important piece of pond equipment, a recirculating pump aerates the water for fish and nearly all plants, discourages mosquitoes, and keeps unpleasant odors at bay.

The trick of buying a liner is to purchase the right size. The rule of thumb is that the length of the liner should equal the length of the pool plus twice the maximum depth of the pool; the width of the liner should equal the overall width of the pool plus twice the maximum depth. In other words, a 2-foot-deep pool measuring 15×10 feet would call for a 19×14-foot liner. Whatever your calculations, don't try to scrimp by using a liner that is too small, even if it's a matter of inches.

There's some debate about which is easier to install—shell or liner. Let's just say that they're different. A small, simply shaped pond is relatively easy to set up with either one. A large piece of liner can be awkward to handle and will form creases and folds that will be relatively hard to clean later. A big shell shaped like an amoeba with numerous built-in shelves or multiple levels requires some skillful excavation. It is challenging to make such a pond perfectly level, and if you don't, your stones or other edging will always be unstable, allowing the rigid black plastic to poke out.

PUMPS AND FOUNTAINS

Pumps may be the scariest aspect of water gardening because they involve the potentially unfortuitous marriage of electricity and water. Fortunately, modern pump construction and local electric codes mixed with a dollop of common sense make this a nonissue. Let's say you want a perfectly still reflecting pond with no mini-Niagaras or geyser-and-tulip fountains. You'll still need a pump

If you're not sure about designing your own pond, start with a preformed shell. The fountain helps aerate the water while adding a pleasant sound.

(and maybe a filter) to aerate the water for fish, nearly all plants, and to discourage mosquitoes and (need we say this?) stench. You could buy an external pump similar to those used with swimming pools, but they're ugly, noisy, and not at all practical for backyard water gardening. We're only talking here about submersible pumps.

To choose a pump of the right size, you'll need to calculate the capacity of your pond (how much water it holds) and the demands of any other features such as waterfalls, fountains, and filters. The latter two are sold with fairly clear instructions as to their requirements, so you'll only need to get that calculator out in regard to the first two, capacity and waterfalls.

The most accurate method of finding your pond's capacity is to attach a flow meter to your faucet when you first fill the pond (a one-time expense), or to compute the capacity based on how long it takes to fill a container of a certain size (say a 5-gallon bucket) compared with how long it takes to fill the pond with the hose turned on at the same rate. Unfortunately, most of us have the pond filled long before we think of this.

For a square or rectangular pond, multiply length times width times depth for cubic feet, then multiply again by 7.5 for the number of gallons your pond holds. For a circular pond, square the diameter, multiply by depth, and then by 5.9. Oval pond? Multiply length by width by depth times 6.7. Treat a free-form pond similarly: Multiply average length times average width times depth times 6.7.

A fall is the most common feature for a water garden, whether it's a stream spewing from a lion's head into an elegant tiled raised pond or a you-*can*-fool-Mother-Nature cascade burbling into a wildlife pond. In either case, you need to know how much water your pond holds and how high the water must be lifted before it tumbles down again.

A liner gives you more freedom, allowing you to create the pond shape that fits best into your landscape.

You'll want your pump to recirculate half of this volume every hour for a pleasantly splooshy sound (and for adequate aeration), even more for crashing drama. Another way to consider pump power is by the depth of the water that the pump will have to push over each lip of your fall. For a gentle stream about ½-inch deep, you'll need a pump that cranks out 50 gallons an hour for each horizontal inch of your fall. For one inch of depth, look for a pump that can handle 150 gallons per inch.

It's not as hard as it sounds, since all pumps come with helpful charts on the box, and water-garden dealers (but not the folks at your local hardware store, unless you're *very* lucky) will provide solicitous help. But so you can waltz into the store prepared, let's talk about lift. Also called "head," it's the height to which your pump has to raise the water. The higher it has to lift the water, the wimpier the outflow. A pump that churns out 300 gallons for a 1-foot patio spill may be able to pump only 120 gallons for a 4-foot, in-ground waterfall.

Always err on the side of too big. Water-garden dealers say that return customers always want something larger, whether pond, pump, or koi. Many pumps come with valves that let you control the flow. Others have multiple outlets that let you hook up other features, such as fountains or filters. There are a number of pump manufacturers—Little Giant and Nautilus are common brands—and prices between makers don't vary much. Expect to pay between $65 and $100 for a submersible pump that will move 300 gallons of water up 3 feet per hour. While your wallet is open, you may want to get a mesh container—about $10—to help keep bits of this and that from clogging your pump.

Fountains are pretty much a matter of aesthetic sensibility. Except for the type called bubblers ($40 plus a pump), they're not appropriate for naturalistic

The usual recommendation for ensuring clear, or at least healthy, water is to cover about 60 percent of the pond's surface with plants, such as the water-lilies shown above.

or small ponds, since a brisk wind will whip their spray onto visitors and adjacent landscaping. For small water features, you can rig up a cobblestone reservoir (shallow and safe for children), a wall fountain (from which a piece of statuary gushes water into a formal pool), or the Japanese bamboo *shishi odoshi,* or "stag scarer." All of these can be pulled off with the smallest of pumps.

FILTERS

A bit more technologically challenging than pumps are water filters, which you must consider purchasing if you plan to get heavily into fish. The colorful carp known as koi are especially demanding of clear water. There are two basic types of filters: mechanical models, which trap physical debris, and biological filters, which break down pollutants.

Mechanical filters, which require a pump, suck up decaying plant debris as well as fish waste and uneaten fish food. Ponds smaller than 1,000 gallons can get by with cartridge-type filters, which have a corrugated polyester fitting that looks a lot like a car's oil filter. Various types strain pond waste through foams, fibers, screens, or activated charcoal; they will need to be cleaned weekly or even daily during the height of the season. The mechanism isn't as important as the size, which manufacturers describe on the box in terms of pond capacity; prices for the filter alone run between $50 and $150. (A device gaining in popularity is the skimmer, which you install in the ground next to the pond, with a separate pump. A skimmer removes leaves and other flotsam from the surface, by sucking the debris into something akin to a vacuum-cleaner bag.)

Biological filters don't need water flowing through them as fast as mechanical filters do. Typically, they turn over the water only every four to six hours and can be run on a small auxiliary pump. They work by moving the water through gravel, charcoal, or other media containing beneficial bacteria. The bacteria break down ammonia and nitrites—and ammonia byproducts—into nitrates that your plants can feed on. Prices depend on pond size and range from $100 to over $1,000.

PLANTS AND FISH

Gardeners who install ponds want to create an environment for plants that don't grow on land, and—quite likely—to raise fish or attract wildlife. You should think of many of these plants and animals as living tools. A water garden correctly stocked with these natural filters may not need a mechanical or biological filter.

Submerged plants, similar to ones you see in aquariums, are the workhorses of water gardens, helping to keep your pond chemistry and biology in balance. Plants with floating leaves, such as water-lilies, play an important role by covering the surface of the pond, keeping the water cool so that unsightly algae don't take over.

In addition to plants, water-garden suppliers sell snails, pond janitors that are good at gobbling spent flowers and uneaten fish food that otherwise would decay and foul the water. The black Japanese or trapdoor snail is the one you'll find for sale most often—$10 to $15 a dozen—and it's less likely than others to eat pond plants. Tadpoles, which run $2 to $3 each, can fulfill the same function, and of course in due time become frogs that serenade us and help control the insect population (as do any toads or birds your pond attracts).

The usual recommendation for clear, or at least healthy, water is to cover about 60 percent of the pond's surface with plants such as water-lilies or other species with floating leaves; plant at least one bunch of submerged plants—anacharis, hornwort, and parrot's feather are widely available—per square foot of water surface; and stock at least one scavenger for each square foot of water surface.

DRESSING UP

ORNAMENTS IN THE GARDEN

BARBARA PERRY LAWTON

THE BEST GARDENS are more than plants arranged in artful ways. They also include garden accessories that express the gardener's personality. Sundials, statuary, trellises, benches, gazebos—all these and many other ornamental (and sometimes ornamental *and* practical) items offer ways to add your signature to the garden. Gardens are most interesting—and most enjoyable—when they are personal.

Mail-order and online catalogs, nurseries, garden centers, and hardware, farm, and other retail stores are loaded with products that you can adopt to embellish your garden. Craftsmen may want to design and build their own garden features. Or you may find something among your own or someone else's castoffs that holds real promise as gardening decor. Substituting a child's wagon for a planter is an example of using a found object in the garden. I know of one garden in which an antique tractor was left where it wheezed into silence. The owners created a raised bed around it, planted a grand perennial garden, and now it is known as the Tractor Garden. With found—or abandoned—objects, you're limited only by what you can scrounge and by your daring.

If I were to mention even half of the beautiful and interesting things you can use to enhance your garden, this would be an endless chapter. Instead, I've tried to skip lightly through the forest of available garden ornaments. Study horticulture magazines and catalogs. Drop by local stores. Surf the Web. You're bound to discover objects that will complement your garden.

BENCHES AND OTHER RESTING SPOTS

Chairs, tables, and other garden furniture are practical items, but they can be ornamental as well. Look for examples that match your garden's style—a twig chair may look out of place in a formal garden—and for furniture that is well made and able to withstand outdoor conditions.

Wood benches, chairs, settees, and tables are the first choice of many gardeners selecting outdoor furniture. I choose products made from sustainably

Garden furniture can be practical as well as ornamental. The bench made from a wagon wheel easily withstands outdoor conditions.

harvested woods, such as eastern white cedar and cypress, rather than from woods taken from endangered rain forests. Or look for items made from teak and other woods that have been certified by the Forest Stewardship Council. Many styles are available, from classic English designs to casual Adirondack furniture.

There also has been a resurgence of twig furniture, the ultimate rustic look. Like the look of wicker? Consider faux wicker furniture made of tough, waterproof resin plastics. The only way you can tell it from the real thing is that the furniture won't be frayed or cracked after a year of use. Chairs are about $100, cushions $30.

Don't forget about garden benches made of stone or formed concrete. Strategically placed, they make lovely places to "take five" on a hot day. Equally

Ornamental and functional, a birdhouse makes a welcome addition to the garden.

long lasting is garden furniture made from—you'd never guess—recycled tires. Chair and bench designs vary, and there's something for nearly any setting.

Remember the molded sheet metal chairs of 50 years ago? Like Fiestaware, they're popular once again. You may find an original in a secondhand store, but it's easier to buy one of the new models that are being manufactured.

The top of the line in outdoor furniture is a class I call "living-room furniture for gardens." Elegantly designed and manufactured in molded and worked metals, some upholstered in weather-resistant fabrics, these items lend panache to the garden. High-quality products are pricey—unupholstered chairs begin at $250—but sturdy and handsome.

It's nice to have a table nearby on which to rest a drink. Choose one that matches your chairs and benches, or get something that is an objet d'art in itself—such as an antique nail keg or unusual tree stump. For storage of cushions (a huge selection of replacement cushions is available from Plow & Hearth) and other outdoor gear, look for storage chests or storage benches, which can double as chairs or tables.

GARDEN ORNAMENTS

The category of garden art includes a multitude of glories—and a few questionables. In general, it's probably accurate to say that less is better than more, but there are no rules. It's *your* garden, so if you want a pink flamingo standing dead center in a bed of red salvia, put one there. The choices are unlimited, but

Butterfly hibernation boxes are handsome, but don't be disappointed if they're mostly popular with spiders. Attract butterflies to your garden by adding plants that provide them with food and shelter.

here are a few ornaments that caught my eye.

For walls, there are bas reliefs of cast concrete, metal, and wood that offer pithy sayings, winking peasants, smiling suns, and other images, as well as ornamental planters and lavabos. Both contempory designs and reproductions are available.

Garden statues of cast concrete depict children, cherubs, gnomes, cats, pigs, rabbits, frogs, hedgehogs, pelicans, and lions. There are Asian lanterns, medieval crosses, Buddhas, Apollos, saints, Rhine maidens, obelisks, artichokes, pineapples, and even gastropods, if your garden doesn't have enough snails already.

Other garden statues, many made of metal, give us cranes, dragonflies, butterflies, dancing fairies—even solar-powered glowworms that come to life at night and 2-foot-tall penguins (guaranteed to be "quiet and well-behaved") at $25 a pop. There are whimsical "pebble people," and garden silhouettes—fairies, birds, bugs—made from steel and painted black. The only problem is knowing when to stop.

Bee skeps made of woven straw or twigs are popular with herb gardeners. They aren't expected to contain a hive of bees but do lend an old-fashioned air. 14-inch models cost about $28.

Gazing balls, either resting directly on the ground or sitting on a stand, are again in vogue. Rumored to keep witches away, a 10-inch stainless steel ball costs around $50, a pedestal another $40; a glass ball and stand runs between $50 and $100.

Bee skeps made of woven straw are popular with herb gardeners. They lend an old-fashioned air to the garden.

Don't forget those jig-sawed and painted folk-art figures—elves, flocks of ducks, donkeys and carts, pigs of all sorts as well as other barnyard animals. Flamingoes, too, are part of our folk-art tradition—touted as "authentic American originals." They now come in metal and wood in addition to the traditional plastic. I'd rather see a small flock of pink flamingoes waltzing through a garden bed than a solitary soul standing watch over a lawn. A flurry of six will set you back $39 or $15 for six mini-flamingoes.

Some garden ornaments are more than ornamental. Such multi-purpose garden statuary includes neoclassical maidens with outstretched hands that double as bird feeders, cherubs cuddling birdbaths, and glass calla lilies that collect rainwater for butterflies ($25). Stillbrook sells dew-drop hummingbird feeders ($32), blown-glass spheres that look like colorful fruits when hung in a tree, from a pole, or from the eaves of the house. Ornamental water-faucet knobs are available, as are polyresin bullfrogs and "troutspouts" that channel water at the base of downspouts.

Varmint control is the aim of a number of quasi-ornamental products now on the market. There are horned owls ($25 for a model with a rotating head) and colorful tapes made of Mylar or other plastics that promise to scare off rodents and birds. Sparkling wind socks of shiny Mylar ribbons also claim to frighten garden trespassers; whirligigs on stakes are reputed to discourage moles and voles. Ceramic toad houses—toads not included—start at $15, and slug pubs cost about $30. Beer extra.

If you feel handy and inventive, make your own trellises, such as this pea teepee fashioned from twigs pruned from the garden.

WIND AND WATER FEATURES

Birdsongs aren't the only sounds you'll want in your garden. (You can ensure avian music by including plants that provide food and shelter in your design.) I'm not suggesting you install an outdoor sound system, but that you enliven your aural environment by harnessing wind and water.

Wind chimes top my list for musical charm. My favorites still are the simple metal or bamboo tubes of varying lengths(about $20). There are also mobiles with hanging brass bells ($45) as well as wind chimes made of glass and other materials. When choosing wind chimes, check their tones before you buy, to make sure they suit your ear.

Garden fountains make a music all their own. They come in all sizes, from small tabletop fountains for patios and decks (you can have one for less than $75) to Versailles-like fountains that produce a magnificent roar and splash. New on the market are water sprinklers made of copper and other materials that are not only functional sprinklers but also make water-drop designs in the air. Some have parts that turn with the force of the water. No sound, but what could be more fun on a hot summer day? Prices range from $25 to $125.

PLANT STANDS, TRELLISES, AND GAZEBOS

Manufacturers of garden products seem to have caught on to the fact that it's good business when something useful is also beautiful. The result has been an

explosion of artful solutions to dealing with plants that climb or trail, or that live in containers.

Plant stands are effective on a patio, terrace, or along a path and can be as simple as a stump or as elegant as a wrought iron stand handcrafted by a local artisan. Enchanting are the half-round étagères made of iron. Buy two to encircle a tree trunk or other upright object ($75 each).

You'll throw out your wood stakes after you see the new grow-through hoops, gathering rings, single-stem rings, and linking stakes that will keep dahlias and other tall plants on their feet. Recent designs include finial-topped pyramid trellises with flexible steel legs that let you adjust heights and widths ($15), and metal rods topped with butterflies and fairies ($7.50).

You can construct your own trellis by using bamboo lashed together with traditional hemp twine. (Top the construction with a terra-cotta finial, $12.95.) If you don't feel handy, there are ready-made trellises aplenty to choose from. Wood, metal, and recycled plastic models can be arched or square. Some designs— which qualify as arbors—include gates and serve as entrances to the garden or feature benches for sitting. Prices range from $200 for a wood garden arch to $350 and up for a small wood arbor with a bench; a simple metal arch trellis runs about $200.

Palladian trellises, fan-shaped or rectangular, serve as supports for climbers planted against a house or wall. Half-round trellises can be joined around downspouts or mailbox posts to support vines. Vegetable gardeners may want to look for ladderlike wood trellises made to bear heavy loads of melons and squash ($20).

Gazebos are at the high end of the price scale and rightly so, for many of these are jewels of design and construction. They make superb summerhouses, places to enjoy an iced drink as you survey the garden. (If your portfolio is doing well, a 6-foot-tall woven willow wigwam for kids is available by mail—for around $375 with shipping.)

LIGHTS

If you don't want to stop using and enjoying your garden when the sun sets, give Selene, the goddess of the moon, some help. There are a range of choices, from comprehensive underground wiring to inexpensive and low-tech alternatives. Here are a few of my favorites in the latter category.

Try a string of ornamental line lights with metal shades punched with stars and other shapes (a string of 10 costs about $35). For a dramatic effect, drape them in small trees.

Solar-powered lights, which come with in-ground spikes or railing mounts, are great for softly defining garden beds and other areas. They go on automatically at dusk and will burn for up to eight hours. (A set of four runs about $165.)

Opposite: To enjoy your garden after dark, add some decorative lights, such as these candle-powered lanterns.

Bamboo tiki lamps, oil-fueled torches on tall stakes, are another way to light the garden or a garden path; metal versions are also available ($45). Kerosene lamps are an old-fashioned alternative. Even prettier are candle-powered sconces and lanterns. Punched-tin lanterns with candles (try citronella candles for bug control) create fascinating light patterns (prices start at $15). Even smaller are steel cones that you fit with tea lights and insert in the soil (a set of three costs $10). And to light your pond or pool, there are floating torches, $25 for 6-inch models.

LABELS, CLOCKS, AND WEATHER DEVICES

Experienced gardeners know that much of garden-making is in the details. That means keeping records—the names of plants, the average temperatures, the prevailing direction of the wind. And despite the advice to "count none but the happy hours," you may want to keep track of time you spend pulling weeds.

Plant labels are functional, but in recent years artists and craftsmen have moved labels into the realm of decorative arts. You'll find handsome garden labels of fired clay, metal, and carved wood. Especially fun for children are the brightly painted ears of corn, pea pods, and other vegetables.

The sundial is the oldest known tool for telling time. Today's versions tend to come with Roman numerals, cherubs, and bronze patinas, but you can find contemporary designs. Old or new, they are handsome focal points in a sunny garden, whether resting on the ground or placed on a pedestal.

The armillary sundial, a handsome construction of metal circles and partial circles mounted with an arrow, is typically made of wrought iron and brass. Inexpensive models begin at $75; more elaborate armillary sundials

Opposite: Plant labels used to be strictly functional, but in recent years artists and craftsmen have moved them into the realm of decorative arts. Right: Old or new, a sundial makes a handsome focal point in a sunny garden.

cost four or five times that much.

Weather vanes, those rooftop sculptures that point into the wind, can be the crowning touch not only of barns but also of toolsheds and other garden structures. And they add an ornamental dimension to weather watching. Designs feature everything from roosters to trumpet-blowing angels. Remember that weather vanes look best when they are in scale with the structures that they top; otherwise, the sky's the limit.

If scaling the roof isn't your idea of fun, you might want to consider a ground-based metal weathervane mounted on a brass rod. Many designs feature wildlife—butterflies, hummingbirds, dragonflies—and are priced at $30.

Temperature is crucial to gardening, so be sure to include thermometers as part of your outdoor decor. Outdoor thermometers now come in terra-cotta, brass, galvanized metal, and other handsome materials. (Classic brass models start at $30.) Some thermometers record both the high and low temperature for each day, a useful feature. And you may want to get a barometer and do a little weather forecasting of your own.

Every gardener should have a rain gauge, but you no longer need to settle for the traditional utilitarian model. Rain gauges, too, have become garden decorations. If a gauge mounted on a brass fish or frog ($15) doesn't appeal to you, decorate a large coffee can and use that as your rain gauge—it will work just as well.

OUTFITTING
THE GARDENER

SYDNEY EDDISON

ONE OF THE BEST THINGS about gardening is that you don't have to take lessons or wear special clothes. You can learn on the job; pick up most of what you need to know from gardening friends and neighbors; read garden books and magazines; and go to lectures and classes to fill in the gaps.

Quite honestly, most of the gardeners of my acquaintance don't care what they look like in the garden. In *The Country Garden* (1970), my all-time favorite gardening book, witty, wonderful, wise Josephine Nuese describes her appearance at the end of a winter walk. (Her walks were scavenger hunts for treasures to bestow upon the garden.)

> What you do now is pray that you don't meet any of your fancy nongardening friends as you trudge along, ballooning bags of rotten wood and pine needles, dragging old branches behind you, your nose running (you forgot the handkerchief), your person disheveled, your head full of spring dreams for next year's garden.

That's what *real* gardeners are all about. If you are a down-on-your-knees grubby gardener, you will wear your oldest and most disreputable garments. If you are a tidy gardener, you can get away with more civilized attire. But whatever your sartorial style, you'll want to be comfortable at all costs. You must be able to lift, bend, stretch, reach, and creep. You must be warm when the weather is cold, cool when it's hot, and dry no matter what the temperature.

SPECIAL CIRCUMSTANCES

Even *real* gardeners must protect themselves from the sun's UVA and UVB rays. Gone are the days of basking until your skin turned a rich copper-tan. Doctors have determined that lengthy exposure to the ultraviolet rays in sunlight is harmful to your health. Nowadays, gardeners are urged to cover themselves with long sleeves, long trousers, and hats—and a high-level sun screen.

Gardening gloves come in an array of colors, styles, and materials. Look for a pair that fits, keeps your hands dry, and allows freedom of movement.

If you are running power equipment, especially a chipper/shredder, you *must* protect your eyes and ears. There are now stylish safety glasses—both clear and tinted—that meet American National Standards Institute (ANSI) guidelines; prices begin at $10. Or you can purchase goggles with impact-resistant lenses for as little as $5. You can use simple earplugs to protect yourself from the roar of motors—a bag of 10 pairs of disposable plugs runs about $5. (If you're not sure what plug will be most comfortable, Gempler's offers an "Earplug Sampler": 40 pairs in eight styles for $21.25 plus shipping.) Basic earmuffs—no radio with high-fidelity stereo—are $10 to $25.

Those of us who live where disease-bearing ticks are a problem have an added incentive to cover up. Wearing light-colored clothing isn't a bad idea either. The tiny deer tick that carries Lyme disease is no bigger than the head of a pin and hard to spot against a dark background. In Canada and northern New England, the blackfly is the spring gardening menace. It's small wonder that bug-baffling gear seems to have been developed where the need is greatest. The Original Bug Shirt Company, of Trout Creek, Ontario, sells a line of lightweight, loose-fitting mesh garments (about $55 for a shirt, $60 for pants). The mesh netting is fine enough to filter out everything from no-see-ums to ticks. A simple head hood, the item most gardeners need, costs between $5 to $15.

In cold, raw weather, staying dry in the garden is as important as staying warm, and I think it actually does pay to buy foul-weather gear. Mine consists of baggy waterproof pants with elastic around the waist and ankles to pull over regu-

Wearing a hat, long-sleeved shirt, long pants, waterproof shoes, and gloves, you are ready for gardening in any weather.

lar trousers. The matching jacket is also loose and baggy, to wear on top of a heavy sweater or jacket. My husband found my outfit at an Army-Navy store, but catalogs catering to the hunting and fishing crowd offer similar getups, as does Gempler's. Heavy-duty, "breathable" rain pants cost about $35, jackets $45, but PVC-over-polyester rain suits begin at $20 for both pants and jacket.

GETTING DOWN

Weeds are not a human health menace, but they are a fact of life in every garden. There are two schools of weeding: the benders and the creepers. Benders remain standing and lean down to pull weeds. My gardening mentor, Helen Gill, was a bender. Five feet tall and of the old school, Helen gardened in a dress. Neither she nor the dress had a waist, so to pull weeds she simply folded her sturdy little body in half—again and again and again.

Creepers move from place to place on all fours. While benders need garments with loose waistbands, creepers need protection for their knees. A confirmed creeper, I usually elect a costume of shirt and long trousers—jeans or light cotton twill pants in warm weather; corduroys in the fall and winter. I have tried kneepads but found them an uncomfortable nuisance. If you want to try them, plan on investing between $10 and $30 for foam-rubber pads; adding a plastic kneecap to protect against stones will add $10.

On my desk is a catalog from the Colonial Williamsburg Foundation. For $58 plus shipping and handling, it will send you its "Innovative Gardener's Pants, brimming with distinctive 18th-century details." These include button fly, big pockets with fold-over button flaps, a waistband that adjusts in back

Rubber boots may make you feel rather clumsy, but they can be useful in cold or wet weather.

with buttoned French tabs, and distinctly 21st-century zippered knee pockets for removable quilted kneeling pads. While purchase of products from the catalog supports a good cause, you should ask yourself if these expensive trousers are any better than your old jeans or corduroys.

TREADING THE PRIMROSE PATH

Even the most casual dressers among us are serious about shoes, gloves, and headgear. Years ago, I had a pair of work shoes that I loved, called "Tyroleans." Blissfully comfortable, they were the ideal shoes for gardening, with leather uppers and soles of some lightweight synthetic material. The soles had ridges that provided traction but didn't collect mud, and the uppers were virtually waterproof. A local shoe-repair shop kept my Tyroleans going for 10 years. But I have never since found a completely satisfactory replacement.

Presently, I garden in soft leather walking shoes, which I ruin at the rate of a pair a year. They are sturdy enough for digging, comfortable, flexible, and lightweight. But they are neither waterproof nor warm enough for cold-weather gardening. I also garden in Wellington boots. A friend found them for me in England, where they cost $8 at an ironmongers—the equivalent of a North American hardware store. They are completely waterproof and, with heavy wool socks, tolerably warm. However, they are also clumsy and fairly heavy, and on this side of the Atlantic they cost anywhere from $65 to $85.

The colorful clogs that look like Hans Brinker's wooden shoes are cute but uncomfortable. I still use mine in the summer to run outside in the wet grass. But I wouldn't dream of working in them. The up-tilted toes are painful. In addition to the clogs, I have a pair of "mud shoes." These are made in Europe from

PVC and are a cut above clogs in terms of usefulness and comfort. The PVC is flexible, durable, and waterproof, but the cleats on the bottom collect horrid little cakes of mud. No amount of scraping gets it off until it dries and falls off all over the kitchen floor.

I have friends who swear by Teva sandals ($40 to $80) with thick soles and tough nylon straps for summer gardening. I found them cool and comfortable, but they don't protect your bare feet from accidental encounters with gardening tools. So, having never found an ideal pair of gardening shoes, I cling to happy memories of my Tyroleans and keep trying out different kinds.

HANDS ON

To balance my failure in the shoe department, I have found the perfect gardening gloves: the Mud Glove, made by a family business, Little's Good Gloves, in Sedona, Arizona. My first pair was sent to me by my gardening niece in California. An unforgettable color purple, they were made of soft, cotton knit coated with textured latex rubber. It was love at first sight. Moreover, they were a perfect fit in size small. They come in small, medium, and large. They come in pink, lilac, yellow, dark blue, green, royal blue, brown, or red, and cost $8. Comfortable and not too inhibiting, the Mud Glove is the next best thing to gardening bare-handed.

Having tried many different kinds of gardening gloves, here are my findings: Cotton gardening gloves are all right if the weather is warm and dry. They succeed in keeping your hands from becoming too much like sandpaper but are useless in cold, wet weather and short-lived in any weather. Cowhide and goatskin gloves are long-wearing but turn stiff and uncomfortable after they have gotten wet and then dried. For my money, the Mud Glove is the hands-down winner.

I don't really like gardening in gloves at all, but if I don't, my thumbs crack. My gardening friend Steve Silk, who suffers from the same complaint, gave me a tip just the other day, which is well worth passing on. He anoints his hands with Dumont No-Crack Day Use hand cream and then puts on surgical gloves. He wears these either under other gloves or on their own for delicate operations like sowing seeds. The latex is thin enough to give you complete sense of touch, and of course, it is waterproof. While you work, the cream does its job of moisturizing your skin.

HEADS UP

I belong to the generation that actually wore hats. In 1949, I arrived in England to visit my grandmother complete with a hatbox. My mother had insisted. She adored hats and looked very fetching in them, especially those with broad brims. I used to fancy myself in them, too. But not for gardening.

Finding a comfortable hat that keeps the sun off your face but doesn't get in the way isn't easy. You just have to try different styles. While I love the look of the wide-brimmed Panama straw hats, they are tiresome in the garden. They

A gardening hat protects you from the sun as well as from insects. And it is much safer and more effective to spray insect repellent on the hat than on your skin.

catch on clothing and get in the way. Nor do I like baseball caps. They make tufts of my short hair stick out above my ears like a clown.

The closest I've come to the perfect garden hat is made of 100 percent cotton and has a narrow brim that can be turned up in back so that it doesn't catch on my collar. It is as light as a feather and machine washable. My present garden hat is reversible—bright orange on the outside, orange-and-white print on the inside—and came from the Gap. My husband got it for me last year to match my color scheme for the pots on the terrace. L.L. Bean carries a similar hat for $17.

Searching for a suitable gardening hat is not as frivolous a pursuit as it seems. A hat not only provides protection from the sun but also from insects. And it is much safer and more effective to spray insect repellent on the hat than on your skin. Daylily buffs like me often "break bloom" in the evening, rather than "deadhead" in the morning. At sundown, the blossoms are still fresh and beautiful, and snapping them off is a pleasure. By morning, they will have closed and be slimy and horrid to remove. The only downside to breaking bloom is that the mosquitoes are out in force at that time of day. But spraying my little cloth hat goes a long way toward keeping them at bay.

When work is done, I divest myself of all my repellent-sprayed gardening clothes in the laundry room, stuff everything into the washing machine, and check my person for ticks. Then I repair to a bathtub full of heavenly smelling lavender bath salts. The gardener dressed as nature made her.

BOOKS AND MORE FOR GARDENERS

SALLY WILLIAMS

THERE IS A DAUNTING PLETHORA of data available to North American gardeners, information both helpful and inspiring. And far too much for anyone to tackle head-on. Scores of garden periodicals are published each year; thousands of garden books sit on library and store shelves; millions of web sites appear on the computer screen when you enter "gardening" in a search engine. The first thing we all need are tools to help us find our way through today's information glut to just the right book, just the right article, just the right web site.

SOURCES OF SOURCES

I recommend beginning with resources that help find resources. There are several equivalents for gardeners, but a good place to start is *Gardening by Mail* (5th edition, 1997). It is an annotated directory of sources, mostly for products that can be purchased by mail, plus lists of books, magazines, catalogs, com-

No Englishman would dig with a shovel.

By preference, I wouldn't dig with anything else.

And I also use a shovel to shovel with. . . .

—Charles Elliott, *The Transplanted Gardener,* 1995

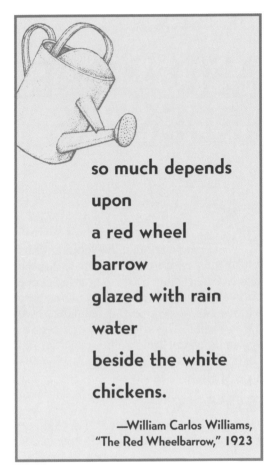

so much depends

upon

a red wheel

barrow

glazed with rain

water

beside the white

chickens.

—William Carlos Williams,
"The Red Wheelbarrow," 1923

puter programs, videos and web sites, libraries, horticultural organizations, and plant and seed sellers. With *Gardening by Mail,* which editor Barbara Barton revises every few years, you'll find sources of information for any regional need or special topic. Interested in garden restoration? In buying ergonomic tools? In touring gardens or joining the Rock Garden Society? It's all there.

You'll also want to find relevant books and periodical articles. Books bring information together in a coherent way and are easy to use. Periodicals—journals, magazines, newsletters, and newspapers that are published regularly—contain a broad range of topics and provide current and timely data. Although computerized media are gaining in acceptance among gardeners, we still love books and magazines! But how do you find a book about Thomas Jefferson's garden at Monticello, or an up-to-date article on growing apples organically?

For this you need an index, a catalog, or list of citations of books and published articles that you can search in various ways, usually by author or topic, such as "old roses," or by plant name, title of book reviewed, or all of the above. Some magazines publish indexes to their own articles, but many do not. While general indexes and databases that include a few national garden magazines, such as the *Readers' Guide to Periodical Literature,* are available in large libraries, searchable topics tend to be very broad, and many worthy articles are overlooked. Let me tell you about two of the best-kept secrets in the world of garden literature.

First—and here I admit to tooting my own horn—is *Garden Literature: An Index to Periodical Articles and Book Reviews,* an index devoted to gardening magazines. I began it in 1991 partly because I couldn't find the information I wanted. *Garden Literature* is an annual listing of articles in a dozen of the leading horticulture magazines published in the U.S. and U.K. Each article is listed under author and under multiple topics, including plant names, names of gardens, and garden designers; reviews (books, software, and videos) are listed by author or creator and title.

Second, you can locate relevant articles and books through Plant Information Online, a database compiled by the Andersen Horticultural Library (Minnesota Landscape Arboretum, University of Minnesota) and available on its web site (http://plantinfo.umn.edu). It is both an index to pictures of plants published in books and magazines and an excellent source of information, since most books and magazine articles include illustrations. The web site also contains sources for some 70,000 plants and seeds.

The premier U.S. publisher of garden books is Timber Press (www.timberpress.com). Others to look for are Chelsea Green, Fulcrum Publishing, Houghton Mifflin, Rodale Press, Sunset Books, Taunton Press, and Ten Speed Press. If you are unsure about a book's merits, buy from bookstores that screen their wares for quality. The mail-order bookstores of the American Horticultural Society, Brooklyn Botanic Garden, and the American Nurseryman Publishing Company carefully select their stock. You may want to shop online for the best price. If you don't require new books the instant they're published, you'll find even bigger discounts from Edward R. Hamilton, Bookseller, who sells remaindered books (www.edwardrhamilton.com).

FILLING AN INFORMATION TOOLBOX

There are basic tools no gardener would be without—trowel, spade, hoe, and rake come to mind—but there is less agreement among gardeners about which tools for the mind, books and periodicals, are essential. It depends on where you live and what kind of garden you tend. You may want to create a balanced horticultural library, with books and periodicals on all aspects of gardening; or you may want information only about a particular aspect of horticulture, such

A gardener not wholly herbivorous

From wilting was out to deliver us.

With blood, sweat and toil

She composted the soil

And made even the lilies carnivorous.

—Cecil Beaton, from Hugo Vickers' biography *Cecil Beaton*, 1985

as heirloom roses. Whatever your plan, wherever your location, keep in mind that gardening information has two basic functions: to inform and to inspire. Ask of any tool you are considering which of the two is its main purpose, and ask yourself which of the two you seek.

The general periodicals I can't do without are *The American Gardener, The Avant Gardener,* Brooklyn Botanic Garden's handbooks and its *Plants & Gardens News, Fine Gardening, The Garden, Garden Design, Gardens Illustrated, Horticulture, Allen Lacy's Homeground, HortIdeas, Hortus,* and *Pacific Horticulture,* plus magazines for my special interests, regional needs, and international desires. Several of these are available online, usually modified in scope, and some are in the public library.

You may be surprised at how many periodicals are available. Did you know that there are publications devoted exclusively to growing chile peppers, to mushrooms, to bamboo, to ivy? Extensive lists of periodicals appear in *Gardening by Mail* and in *Ulrich's International Periodicals Directory,* which is available in public libraries. Many garden web sites also maintain lists of garden periodicals, both general and specialized, but you'll have to visit more than one to compile a good list

As for books, here are my suggestions for a core collection of "tried and true" in-print works. The absence of a title does not mean the book lacks merit, nor does its inclusion mean that it is the only worthy one. In fact, there are hundreds of great books waiting for the right home. I hope this minimal selection stimulates you to search for them!

> With a hydrant and hose, of course, one can water faster ... in a relatively short time we have watered not only the beds, but the lawn, the neighbour's family at their tea, the passersby, the inside of the house, all the members of the family, and ourselves most of all.
>
>  —Karel Čapek, *The Gardener's Year,* 1929

GENERAL REFERENCE. For comprehensive information about gardens and gardening, you can't go wrong with *The Brooklyn Botanic Garden Gardener's Desk Reference* (1998), *Rodale's All-New Encyclopedia of Organic Gardening* (1997), or *Wyman's Gardening Encyclopedia* (1986). Rita Buchanan's *Taylor's Master Guide to Landscaping* (2000) is an excellent one-volume guide to garden design.

PLANTS. If you can have only one book on plants (impossible for most gardeners) you should have the *American Horticultural Society A-Z Encyclopedia of Garden Plants* (1997). "Must-haves" for digging deeper are Allan Armitage's *Garden Perennials: A Color Encyclopedia* (2000), and *Trees and Shrubs: An Illustrated Encyclopedia* (1997) by Michael A. Dirr.

Annuals and bulbs are covered well in *Annuals with Style: Design Ideas From Classic to Cutting Edge* (2000) by Thomas Christopher and Michael A. Ruggiero, and *Taylor's Guide to Bulbs* (2001) by Barbara W. Ellis. Native plants are well served in the *New England Wild Flower Society Guide to Growing and Propagating Wildflowers of the United States and Canada* (2000) by William Cullina. Herb mavens say the new bible is *The Big Book of Herbs* (2000) by gurus Arthur O. Tucker and Thomas DeBaggio. A good combo for edibles is *Burpee: The Complete Vegetable and Herb Gardener* (1997) by Karan Davis Cutler, and William Woys Weaver's *Heirloom Vegetable Gardening* (1997).

To find sources for purchasing specific species and cultivars, consult the Andersen Horticultural Library's *Source List of Plants and Seeds* (5th edition, 1999) or its web site (www.arboretum.umn.edu/library); the Seed Savers Exchange's inventories of nonhybrid flowers, herbs, vegetables, and fruits (www.seedsavers.org); and *Cornucopia II* (1998), an exhaustive list of hybrid and open-pollinated vegetable cultivars. Many plant societies, such as the American Rose Society, regularly publish definitive lists of plant names and sources.

GARDEN HISTORY. Garden history is an aspect too often overlooked by gardeners. An understanding of our roots does much to enhance the enjoyment of our gardens and the landscape around us. Alas, my one-volume candidate, Julia S. Berrall's *The Garden: An Illustrated History from Egypt to the Present Day* (1966), is out of print, but is so good that it's worth looking for in used book-

> **Seed starting, like child raising, is attended by innumerable theories.**
>
> —Josephine Nuese,
> *The Country Garden*, 1970

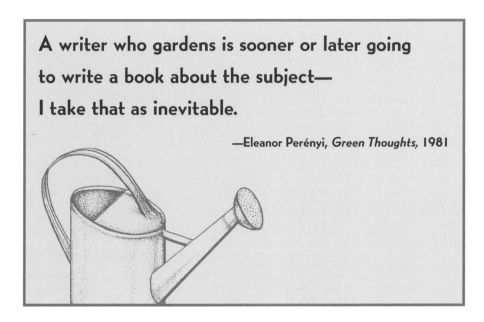

> # A writer who gardens is sooner or later going to write a book about the subject— I take that as inevitable.
>
> —Eleanor Perényi, *Green Thoughts*, 1981

stores (or select one of the many editions offered online through Bibliofind, www.bibliofind.com). *An Illustrated History of Gardening* (1998) by Anthony Huxley will get you thinking about garden tools and techniques, and Michael Weishan's *The New Traditional Garden* (1999) will introduce you to America's garden history. To dig deeper, read classics *Early American Gardens: "For Meate or Medicine"* (1970) by Ann Leighton; *Keeping Eden* (1992) edited by Walter T. Punch; and *The Golden Age of American Gardens* (1991) by Mac Griswold and Eleanor Weller.

GARDEN VISITS. Important in any information toolbox are resources for visiting gardens, which are sources of inspiration and learning. *The Garden Tourist* is one of the first publications I renew annually because it lists flower shows and garden tours as well as gardens to visit. The Garden Conservancy's *Open Days Directory* (www.gardenconservancy.org) is always with me as well. I also rely on the *National Geographic Guide to America's Public Gardens* (1998) and regional guidebooks published by Michael Kesend Publishing, Mitchell Beazley (Europe), Princeton Architectural Press (U.S. and Europe), Random House Australia, Sasquatch Books, and Trafalgar Square.

GARDENING ONLINE

How do you wade through the mire of so many useful (and some not so useful) online garden web sites? Especially when sites are here today and gone tomorrow? The good news is that it takes just one or two sites to link you to thousands of other sites. One that does this well is Gardening Launch Pad (www.gardeninglaunchpad.com), which has nearly 4,500 links, many noncommercial, arranged alphabetically by subject.

Also take a look at the "Gardener's Guide to Finding Answers on the Internet," which is posted on the Garden Gate site (http://garden-gate.prairienet.org), an old favorite gateway. It introduced me to PlantAmerica's extensive illustrated plant database (http://plantdb.plantamerica.com), which utilizes search engines to collect web citations that link to its plant pages. And check the U.S. Department of Agriculture's database (http://plants.usda.gov) or the "Pest Alerts" section on the Brooklyn Botanic Garden web site (www.bbg.org) for invasive species to avoid when you make plant selections. Another superb resource is Ohio State University's Plant Facts (http://plantfacts.ohio-state.edu), a searchable database connecting scores of U.S. and Canadian university and government institutions—instant access to 20,000 pages of extension-service fact sheets and bulletins.

You can get general and regional gardening tips, articles, and online shopping by visiting commercial sites such as Gardennet (www.gardennet.com). If you want to avoid the "noise" of advertising, try the sites of the American Horticultural Society (www.ahs.org) and Brooklyn Botanic Garden.

Most commercial firms—both manufacturers and retailers—now have web sites, usually with their own name as the site address (for example, www.ames.com or www.gardentoolsofmaine.com). If you don't know a company's web address, search the company name in a search engine, such as google (www.google.com) or yahoo (www.yahoo.com), or just type in the company's name plus .com. Most times, you'll find exactly what you're looking for.

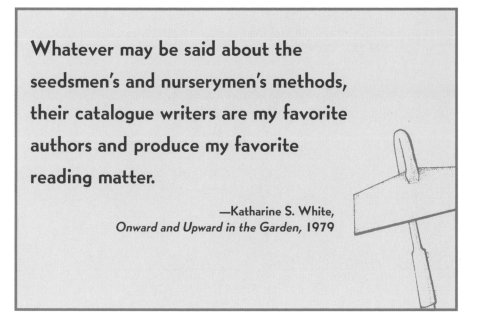

Whatever may be said about the seedsmen's and nurserymen's methods, their catalogue writers are my favorite authors and produce my favorite reading matter.

—Katharine S. White,
Onward and Upward in the Garden, 1979

EXPERTS PICK THEIR CAN'T-LIVE-WITHOUT GARDEN TOOLS

GARDEN TOOLS ARE SO IRRESISTIBLE that your first purchase probably should be a building for storing what you buy. None of our experts lists a garden shed, which suggests that most of them can't fit a car into their garage. Nevertheless, here are their tool choices, the six items they absolutely, positively couldn't do without.

LINDA YANG lives on one fortieth of an acre only five blocks from Rockefeller Center in New York City, yet boasts of a birch "grove" (five trees), a bamboo "forest" (six plants), and a lilliputian lotus pond. A prolific writer, her newest book is *Topiaries & Espaliers* (1999).

COMFORTABLE GARDEN PANTS. I own two pairs of threadbare, baggy pants for gardening. Both have a plethora of pockets for carrying an astonishing assortment of items.

JAPANESE BONSAI PRUNER. Mine has elongated and pointed blades, practical for nearly everything I want to cut.

RAIN GAUGE. It tells me how much moisture has *really* touched the ground.

ADJUSTABLE HOSE NOZZLE. I use the strong jet stream to wash away both city dust and insect eggs and larvae.

PLASTIC-COATED NETTING. Crucial to a clematis addict like me, netting is also good for deterring birds from plants I'd rather they didn't perch on or dig among.

DUSTPAN AND BRUSH. They're essential for cleaning the stone paths and for relocating my neighbor's hateful ailanthus leaves.

DAVID S. DAEHNKE, Executive director of the Reeves-Reed Arboretum in Summit, New Jersey, is also the host of a radio-show ("The Gardening Guru")

Opposite: If you are a down-on-your-knees, nose-in-the-dirt gardener or if your growing takes place on a patio or deck, hand tools are for you. The hand trowel is the backbone of this family of implements.

Left: A rain gauge tells you how much rain has really fallen, and therefore how much you need to water.

Opposite: A file is essential to keep tools sharp, from lawnmower and pruner blades to saws and spades.

and maintains a web site (www.gardeningguru.org). He tends a half acre in Mahwah, New Jersey, and grows everything from fruits and vegetables to exotic specimen plants.

FELCO PRUNER #7. This pruner has rotating handles, which reduces the number of calluses.

NURSERY SPADE. I own a "King of Spades," a 6-pound, one piece, all-steel spade with a rubber footrest and YD-handle.

SWEDISH BRUSH AX. Mine has a long handle like a standard ax and a C-shaped blade. I use it to cut through brush and small trees.

SOAKER HOSE. Mine is the type that can be laid on the ground and covered with mulch. I conserve water by putting it where it is needed, and the hose is made from recycled rubber. A double winner.

FILE. It's essential to keep tools sharp, from lawnmower and pruner blades to saws and spades.

MANTIS TILLER. This is simply a great, lightweight tool with several attachments for all-around garden use.

CAROLINE DEWILDE, whose formal title at the New York Botanical Garden is Commercial Horticulture Coordinator and Instructor, lives in Goshen, New York, and gardens on a hill. Her next project is to build a new bed for interesting woody plants that can withstand both harsh, droughty conditions and deer.

TROWEL. Make sure it's a sturdy one.

LIGHTWEIGHT PRUNER. I use a plastic model with anvil blades made by Henckels. Some people don't like anvil blades, but if they are sharp, they cut cleanly.

FISKARS PRUNING STIK. Expandable to 10 feet, it's lightweight and easy to adjust, perfect for reaching up or down to remove or trim small branches. A great help to those of us who suffer from back problems.

FISKARS POWER-GEAR ANVIL LOPPERS. This is another tool useful for extending pruning reach just beyond where hand pruners can go.

SWAN-NECKED HOE. Ever since I bought one, I rarely use a standard hoe. It's small-headed and easy to maneuver in flower beds.

NURSERY SPADE. Mine is narrower than a traditional spade, perfect for working in small spaces. I ruined one or two until I looked for top quality. This is no place to economize.

RITA BUCHANAN gardens in rural Connecticut and has an acre filled with perennials, shrubs, and groundcovers, as well as a vegetable garden and a greenhouse. Her latest book is *Taylor's Master Guide to Landscaping* (2000), but she's taking a writing sabbatical to build a studio to house her other passions of spinning, knitting, weaving, and basketry.

FOUR-TINE DIGGING FORK. Forks make digging a pleasure. They're ideal for lifting and dividing perennials, but not for digging out rocks. I've bent many tines and broken two handles that way.

HONDA F2 I 0, 5 HP ROTOTILLER. I use a tiller to turn my dirt into soil. Mine is a real workhorse that still starts on the first pull after 14 years of use.

PROFESSIONAL-GRADE BYPASS PRUNING SHEARS. Cutting, shearing, trimming, pruning, you name it—these shears do the job.

METAL BOW SAW. I use one with a 21-inch replaceable blade to cut limbs or trees up to 4 inches. It works almost as fast as a chain saw, and it's safer.

BEARCAT CHIPPER/SHREDDER WITH 8 HP HONDA ENGINE. I feed it brush, leaves, vines, and stalks, and it spits out flakes the size of breakfast cereal. I make designer compost this way.

GLOVES. I never garden bare-handed. My current favorite is the Mud Glove; one pair lasts all season, increases my grip, protects me, and goes through the laundry with my jeans.

GORDON HAYWARD lives in an 18th-century house set on one acre in southern Vermont. (You can see his gardens at www. haywardgardens.com.) His latest book is *Stone in the Garden* (2001), and when he's not gardening or writing about gardening, he designs gardens, lectures about gardens, and leads tours of gardens.

PLASTIC TARPAULIN. I have at least eight of them—the smallest is 8×10 feet—which I spread when I prune, rake leaves, and weed. Then I pull the loaded tarp to the compost pile.

FELCO #2 PRUNER. These indispensable shears are everyone's favorite for a reason: They are easily sharpened, they're adjustable, and you can get replacement parts. Avoid knockoffs.

16-FOOT APPLE LADDER. Mine, from the Lynn Ladder Company, is light and sturdy and tapers toward a single stout point that I can rest in the crotch of two branches.

GOATSKIN GLOVES. The best gloves manufactured anywhere are made by the Green Mountain Glove Company in Randolph, Vermont.

STRAIGHT-NOSED SPADE. I use mine every single day. I keep the high-carbon blade sharp with a diamond sharpening tool, and that keen edge makes all the difference.

Opposite: Plastic netting helps deter animals from eating plants. Right: Homemade or store-bought hot caps, or cloches, protect tender plants from the elements in early spring and in fall.

DUTCH 5-CUBIC-FOOT PLASTIC TUB WHEELBARROW. This wheelbarrow—it has a tubular steel frame and weighs only 26 pounds—is easy to maneuver and empty, and stands up to big jobs.

MARK ADAMS lives in rural New York, where he grow plants—more than 3 million a year—for wholesale greenhouses; he also writes a garden column for the Millbrook, New York, newspaper and "gardens on the side." He specializes in vegetables and new annual flowers.

MANTIS TILLER. If I have a free hour, it lets me prepare a small spot in my garden for planting.

WATER-JUG HOT CAPS. I make them by cutting the bottoms off gallon plastic water jugs and removing the cap for air circulation. They go over my lettuce in early spring, then get moved to the tomato plants in May.

YELLOW THING. That's what I call the fan-shaped breaker that I attach to the trigger nozzle on my garden hose. The trigger nozzle is for washing cars; the yellow thing is for watering plants.

PAGE-A-DAY DIARY. I record everything: dates, weather, varieties, problems, and successes. It's the best way to continually enhance your gardening experience.

TOMATO CAGES. I use cone-shaped wire supports not only on tomatoes but also on peppers, beans, and flowers to keep them upright and to save space.

GREENHOUSE. Mine covers four acres, but even a tiny one can be used for starting plants from seed. That opens up a vast world of interesting varieties you can't buy in garden centers.

LAUREN SPRINGER has designed gardens for the Denver Botanic Gardens and is an award-winning writer and photographer; her most recent book is *Pas-*

The swan-necked hand cultivator from Korea can do anything from scratching out weeds to scooping up soil.

sionate Gardening (2000). She lives on 115 acres in northern Colorado and maintains a garden filled with native perennials, dwarf conifers, bulbs, roses, fruits, and vegetables.

FELCO #8 PRUNER. I keep it in a holster on my belt so as not to lose it, and I have two pairs: One is always too dull to use.

NARROW TROWEL. Mine is made from one piece of metal—all the others I tried bent when I used them in my clay and rocks.

ASPARAGUS KNIFE. I buy inexpensive knives and have several since I'm constantly losing them. They're ideal for weeding.

DIBBLE. Mine is made of high-quality steel. I use it for planting small bulbs, about 5,000 each year.

THREE-INCH AUGER DRILL BIT. Perfect for power-drilling the holes for the 1,000 large bulbs I plant every year.

RAKE. I use a rubber-tined model, so I can clean up my beds and borders in spring without damaging the new growth of the emerging bulbs and perennials.

DAN HEIMS, who owns Terra Nova Nurseries (www.terranovanurseries.com), lives nine minutes from downtown Portland, Oregon, on a tree-covered third-acre lot. He's filled it with woodland plants, perennials, and exotica. He's also writing the "ultimate *Heuchera* book" but still finds time to travel the world to collect plants.

ARS SWITCHBLADE BYPASS PRUNER. The second this baby hit my hands, my Felcos were in the garbage. They weigh less, have sharper, stronger blades, and are ergonomically designed.

ARS ADJUSTABLE POLE PRUNER. Imagine an amazingly light, variable length pole pruner (from 6 to 12 feet) with full twisting action and an ergonomic hand-grip. Japanese steel rules for strength and sharpness.

ARS PROFESSIONAL HEDGE SHEARS. My landscape crew used them daily for a whole season before they needed sharpening—that's 40 years of homeowner use! They're light and strong. Don't buy cheap knockoffs—they will break.

WARREN HOE. The triangular head provides three weeding points, two for smaller weeds and one for deep-rooted ones. Length and effectiveness beat any other hoe. It's also easy for row making. Mine is made by Ames.

H.M. LEONARD SOIL KNIFE. This unbreakable digging knife/trowel/root cutter/multi-use tool comes with a leather scabbard good for macho gardeners of both sexes.

ENGLISH LOC-CHAIN. Strong and invaluable for tying and training vines and wayward branches, Loc-Chain is black, UV-stabilized, and hides well in plants. Cut a piece and it interlocks with any piece of the chain. You'll find a thousand uses in the garden.

TOVAH MARTIN, who lives in a small Connecticut town, has many gardens, including two 80-foot borders planted with heirlooms and a vegetable bed filled with burgundy and blue-gray vegetables. Her patio is dense with potted dahlias, and her 1810 house is also filled with plants. Martin is the garden editor at *Victoria* magazine; her latest book is Brooklyn Botanic Garden's *Old-Fashioned Flowers* (2000).

GLOVES. Not all gardeners swear by them, but for someone who gets poison ivy and is prone to skin problems, they're essential. Mine are a kid's size, cotton, and fit, well, like a glove.

HAND TOOLS. I couldn't do without my froe, a hand cultivator from Asia with a long, swan-necked, elliptical blade that can do anything from scratching out weeds to scooping up soil. My favorite trowel is a heavy, old-fashioned version with a wood handle and a wide blade.

WATERING CAN. For outdoors, I swear by a 2-gallon all-metal model with a rose.

WHEELBARROW. I can't do without my True Temper midget model. It's just my size and makes light work of the worst lugging.

OLD COTTON SHOWER CURTAIN. Mine is covered with mildew stains, but it's great for cleaning up leaves and everything else in the garden.

SHOVEL. I swear by a pointed, short-handled "ladies" shovel. Mine is an antique with a wooden D-handle and covered by worn red paint.

TED MARSTON lives on a sloped half acre bordering Lake Washington in suburban Seattle, where he has created multiple rock and water gardens and uses his greenhouse to grow thousands of annuals, perennials, orchids, and tropical bloomers. After years working in commercial horticulture, Marston now spends most of his time "really gardening."

PRUNING SHEARS. I prefer Felco shears because they're superbly engineered and don't wear out.

GREENHOUSE. Is a greenhouse a tool? In any case, it expands what I can do in the garden and gives me a place to work when it's nasty outside.

PROPAGATION MATS. For someone like me who wants to grow his own plants, heating mats are wonderful for providing the constant warmth that seeds and cuttings need.

SPRINKLING SYSTEMS. Despite what most people believe, it sometimes doesn't rain in Seattle for several months in summer. Having a permanent watering system saves time—and my lugging hoses.

TROWEL. My favorite was an all-aluminum, all-one-piece model that I lost after 15 years of use. It fit my big paw well. I'm still looking for a replacement.

SOIL-PREPARATION TOOLS. To keep my list to six, my last choice would be a portmanteau of tools: a good garden rake with sturdy teeth, an old-fashioned hoe that can be sharpened forever, a narrow-bladed spade, and a spading fork. Each would be custom-designed for my height and hands, would have shafts that never break or separate, and blades and tines that never rust.

WALTER NELSON is a horticulture educator with Cornell Cooperative Extension in south-central New York and gardens on 27 acres, "where bees make honey from the best goldenrod around." His vegetable garden measures 7,000 square feet, and perennial borders surround the house. And he writes a gardening column for the *Star Gazette.*

BUCKET BOSS. This carry-all (it's a cover for a 5-gallon plastic pail with pockets inside and out) is great for hauling small garden tools.

GARDEN CART. A garden cart is much better than a wheelbarrow because it holds so much more and is much less likely to tip.

PENKNIFE. There are always dozens of reasons for having a *sharp* penknife in your pocket.

FLOATING ROW COVERS. These protect tender plants from a late frost, give strawberries a head start, and give me another two weeks of tomatoes and zucchini. And they exclude critters like spinach leaf miners and cucumber beetles.

KOREAN HAND PLOW. It is shaped like a moldboard plow with an 8-inch face and looks like something one might find in a martial arts store. I have two, one on a 12-inch handle for work while kneeling, and one on a 4-foot handle for use while standing. Both grub out deep-rooted weeds better than anything I have tried.

SCUFFLE HOE. Mine is 30 years old and has a metal handle, which creates a pleasant clicking sound as I scuff it back and forth over the soil surface.

KIP SMITH gardens in a "mature" suburban/urban area of Detroit, growing mostly herbs, perennial flowers, and other ornamentals and fruits. An advanced master gardener, Smith often lectures on herbs.

FISKARS LIGHTWEIGHT, NONSTICK TROWEL. When I first received this space-age, glass-filled polymer trowel I thought it would chip and break, but it has held up to all sorts of abuse. It doesn't even rust when left outside all winter.

WINGED WEEDER. This oddly shaped tool comes with either long or short handles. It is excellent for quick weeding of vegetable beds.

A greenhouse extends the growing season in colder areas and gives gardeners a place to do chores when it's nasty outside.

THE MUD GLOVE. These are great—the only gloves I've ever really liked. I can feel what I am doing, yet they're waterproof—I can just hose them off.

THREE-TINED HAND CULTIVATOR. Be sure you get a strong one—mine is made by Ames—because wimpy, cheaply built versions are a waste of money.

FLORIAN PRUNER. The ratchet device gives me extra cutting power, yet they're easy on the hands.

WILLING HUSBAND. Mine moves and mixes compost, digs the large holes, builds trellises, planters, and garden beds. While he feels greatly underappreciated, he responds well to an occasional kind word and continues his serviceability with minimum upkeep. I bring him in during the winter and severe summer storms.

LYNN STEINER lives on an old farm 30 miles northeast of St. Paul, Minnesota, and she grows annuals, perennials, shrubs, vegetables, and herbs. Steiner is also a writer, photographer, and the editor of *Northern Gardener,* the official publication of the Minnesota State Horticultural Society.

FELCO PRUNER. Pruning is one of my favorite gardening tasks. I always have my pruner with me.

FOLDING PRUNING SAW. Mine is a 10-inch model. I use it to get into the tight spots at the base of my shrubs when I'm thinning.

PLASTIC TOOL BUCKET. It's nothing fancy, just a simple three-compartment handled bin I got at Target, but it's just the right size, weight, and price to fit my needs.

Some tools that are popular with many expert gardeners: a Felco pruner, a folding pull saw, and the perfect pair of gardening gloves.

GARDEN PANTS WITH BUILT-IN KNEEPADS. Not really a tool in the true sense of the word, but I wouldn't (or couldn't anymore) garden without them.

WEED BUCKET. I make sure I always have a weed bucket tucked into a corner of the garden so I'm not tempted to lay weeds or clippings in the garden. I use a large black nursery container.

WATERING WAND. I keep mine connected to the hose. The gentle spray doesn't disturb young plants, and it's great for reaching the back areas of gardens and hanging baskets.

TOM WILHITE lives in Marin County, just north of San Francisco, and tends a small urban garden filled with ornamentals and herbs. The senior editor of the latest edition of Sunset's *Western Garden Book* (2001), the horticultural bible for his region, he's just begun working on a book on ornamental grasses.

BYPASS PRUNING SHEARS. Buy bypass, not anvil, shears. I've tried others, but I always come back to Felco.

ONE-PIECE ALUMINUM TROWEL. It's lightweight and strong, and you don't have to worry about a weak joining of the shaft to the blade. Pick one with a rubber grip.

WEEDING TOOL. Mine has a straight shank with a sharp-notched point. It digs straight down along taproots and loosens soil around them. Again, single-piece construction is best.

LEATHER GLOVES. I'm always tempted to leave them in the shed, but then I remember picking out tiny splinters and trying to scrub stains from my skin and nails.

WATERING CAN. For my container plants, including bonsai, I use water that has been sitting for at least 24 hours, so that the chlorine and other chemicals dissipate. I keep several large watering cans filled and ready.

DIGGING SPADE. I use a spade with a square-edged blade. It's best for most tasks.

PAT STONE lives between a mountain and a creek in western North Carolina and grows vegetables and "a few domesticated flowers just for show." Stone is the founder of *GreenPrints* (www.greenprints.com), which he describes as "the only magazine that shares the human, not how-to side of gardening."

STIRRUP HOE. God's gift to gardeners. It easily cuts on back-and-forth strokes while you're standing practically straight. One drawback: It works great on small weeds but not on big ones.

WHEELBARROW. This choice is all too obvious, and all too essential. It totes compost, manure, mulch, hay, firewood—you name it.

ELECTRIC FENCE. Gardening equals varmints. Nothing un-equals that equation better for me than an electric fence. And I don't even have to turn it on to keep our dogs out; they see the wire and cringe.

POSTHOLE DIGGER. Every time I set up a pea or bean fence or a grape or raspberry trellis, I get out that butterfly-scooped tool and lift out big cylinders of earth. And it's so much fun to use!

ROTOTILLER. Mine's on its last legs, but I only use it to start vegetables each spring and turn under cover crops in the summer.

SENSE OF HUMOR. As gardener Inez Castor once told me, "Keep it oiled and not too sharp; you don't want to hurt yourself. Most of all, keep it handy. You never know when you're going to need it."

AURELIA C. SCOTT has gardened in Massachusetts, California, and New Mexico but now lives in Portland, Maine, where she has a 30×30-foot yard with a view of Casco Bay. When she isn't wearing garden gloves, she writes essays and feature stories about gardening, food, and travel.

CAPE COD WEEDER. The high-carbon knifelike blade with a pointed tip does everything from slicing weeds and loosening packed soil to digging out bindweed, edging garden beds, and aerating compost.

TRANSPLANTING SHOVEL. Its long narrow blade slices roots, digs deep holes, and can be used in perennial beds without disturbing neighboring plants.

AMBIDEXTROUS KITCHEN SCISSORS. My pair has a comfortable rubber-covered handle and long, tough blades that I use for deadheading flowers, harvesting leaf crops, cutting twine, and for pruning all but the woodiest shrubs.

COMPOST BIN. Mine is a 40×30-inch black plastic receptacle that is easily filled, aerated, emptied, and moved. It looks unobtrusively attractive in the fanciest garden setting.

LINED KITCHEN RUBBER GLOVES. They aren't good on the hottest days, but they're essential for working in wet soil and for tasks that demand dexterity.

LONG-BILLED NYLON BASEBALL CAP. It's not as picturesque as a straw hat, but it stays put on windy days and is washable.

MAIL-ORDER AND ONLINE SOURCES

DON'T DESPAIR if you don't live a mile from a well-stocked garden store: Everything you could ever need—or want—is only a postage stamp, telephone call, or computer click away. The firms in this list are among the best, culled from the hundreds and hundreds of companies willing to send you everything from a half dozen peat pots to a Victorian archway.

ACCESS WITH EASE
1755 Johnson, P.O. Box 1150
Chino Valley, AZ 86323
800-531-9479
www.store.yahoo.com/capability
Ergonomic tools

THE AMERICAN BOTANIST BOOKSELLERS
210 W. Pine Street, P.O. Box 532
Chillicothe, IL 61523
309-274-5254
www.amerbot.com
Garden books

AMERICAN WEATHER ENTERPRISES
P.O. Box 14381
San Francisco, CA 94114
800-293-2555
www.americanweather.com
Weather instruments, stations, vanes

ARBOR AND BLOOM
6475 E. Pacific Coast Highway, No. 385
Long Beach, CA 90803
562-426-1100
www.arborandbloom.com
Tools, furniture, accessories

A.M. LEONARD
241 Fox Drive
Piqua, OH 45356
800-543-8955
www.amleo.com
Tools, equipment, supplies

CMS GARDENS
2 Seymour Road
Alcester, Warwickshire B49 6JY
United Kingdom
www.cmsgardens.co.uk
British-made tools

CHARLEY'S GREENHOUSE & GARDEN SUPPLY
17979 State Route 536
Mount Vernon, WA 98273
800-322-4707
www.charleysgreenhouse.com
Greenhouses, indoor gardening supplies

THE CULTIVATION STATION
23529 Little Mack
St. Clair Shores, MI 48080
810-775-9485
www.thecultivationstation.com
Hydroponic equipment, supplies

DAVID PARTRIDGE, COPPICE CRAFTSMAN
5 Kiln Close, Corfe Mullen
Wimborne, Dorset BH21 3UR
United Kingdom
http://freespace.virginnet.co.uk/wattle.hurdles
Handcrafted hazel trellises, chairs, baskets

**DIRT WORKS ORGANIC
GARDENING SUPPLY**
6 Dog Team Road
New Haven, VT 05472-4000
800-769-3856
www.dirtworks.net
Soil amendments, compost products,
fertilizers

DRIPWORKS
190 Sanhedrin Circle
Willits, CA 95490
800-522-3747
www.dripworksusa.com
Drip-irrigation equipment

THE ECLECTIC GARDENER
5227 Dredger Way
Orangevale, CA 95662
916-987-7490
http://store.yahoo.com/eclecticgardener
Hand tools

ELISABETH WOODBURN, BOOKS, ABAA
P.O. Box 398
Hopewell, NJ 08525
609-466-0522
www.e-woodburnbooks.com
Garden books

FARBER BAG & SUPPLY CO.
8733 Kapp Dr.
P.O. Box 78
Peosta, IA 52068
800-553-9068
www.farberbag.com
Tools, equipment

FLORENTINE CRAFTSMEN, INC.
46-24 28th Street
Long Island City, NY 11101
718-937-7632
http://florentinecraftsmen.com
Handcrafted metal and stone fountains,
statuary, outdoor funiture

GARDEN ARCHES
P.O. Box 4057
Bellingham, WA 98227
800-947-7697
www.gardenarches.com
Cedar, copper, and iron trellises,
arches, gates

GARDEN ARTISANS
Route. 1, Box 1079-Q5
Townsend, GA 31331
912-437-2270
www.gardenartisans.com
Handcrafted garden accessories

GARDENERS EDEN
1699 Bassford Drive
Mexico, MO 65265
800-822-9600
www.gardenerseden.com
Hand tools, accessories

GARDENER'S SUPPLY COMPANY
128 Intervale Road
Burlington, VT 05401
888-833-1412
www.gardeners.com
Tools, equipment, supplies

GARDENSCAPE
2255B Queen Street East, No. 358
Toronto, ON M4E 1G3
Canada
888-472-3266
www.gardenscapetools.com
Hand tools, ergonomic tools, accessories

GARDEN TOOLS OF MAINE
Route 2, P.O. Box 2208
Holden, ME 04429
888-271-2672
www.gardentoolsofmaine.com
Hand tools, accessories

G.I. DESIGNS
700 Colorado Blvd., No. 120
Denver, CO 80206
866-287-8660
http://gidesigns.home.att.net
Handcrafted copper trellises, arbors,
furniture, accessories

GEMPLER'S, INC.
100 Countryside Drive
P.O. Box 270
Belleville, WI 53508
800-382-8473
www.gemplers.com
Commercial-grade tools, equipment

GREEN MOUNTAIN GLOVE GOMPANY
P.O. Box 25
Randolph, VT 05060
802-728-9160
greenmountainglove.com
Gloves

GROW-IT GREENHOUSES
17 Wood Street
West Haven, CT 06516
800-435-6601
www.growitgreenhouses.com
Greenhouses, cold frames, greenhouse
supplies

HARMONY FARM SUPPLY & NURSERY
3244 Highway 116 North
Sebastopol, CA 95472
707-823-9125
www.harmonyfarm.com
Tools, equipment, supplies

HEARTWOOD INTERNATIONAL
141 Heartwood Circle
Afton, VA 22920
800-452-8251
www.heartwoodinternational.com
Garden products made from reclaimed
wood and recycled plastic

THE INTIMATE GARDENER
4215 North Sheridan Road
Chicago, IL 60613
800-240-2771
www.theintimategardener.com
Garden furniture, accessories

KENNETH LYNCH & SONS
84 Danbury Road
P.O. Box 488
Wilton, CT 06897
203-762-8363
www.klynchandsons.com
Metal and cast-stone statuary, fountains,
ornaments

KINSMAN COMPANY, INC.
P.O. Box 428
Pipersville, PA 18947
800-733-4146
www.kinsmangarden.com
Hand tools, trellises, ornaments

LEE VALLEY TOOLS LTD.
P.O. Box 1780
Ogdensburg, NY 13669
800-267-8735
www.leevalley.com
Tools, equipment

LEHMAN'S
P.O. Box 41
Kidron, OH 44636
888-438-5346
www.lehmans.com
Tools, equipment, weather vanes

LILYPONS WATER GARDENS
P.O. Box 10
Buckeystown, MD 21717-0010
800-999-5459
www.lilypons.com
Water-garden supplies

LITTLE'S GOOD GLOVES
P.O. Box 1966
Sedona, AZ 86339
888-967-5548
www.mudglove.com
Gloves, assessories

MASTER GARDEN PRODUCTS
15650 SE Ninth Street
Bellevue, WA 98008-4902
800-574-7248
www.mastergardenproducts.com
Wood furniture, arbors, trellises, planters

MOTUS INC.
39 Nanton Avenue
Winnipeg, MB R3P 0N1
Canada
204-489-8280
www.motus.mb.ca
Ergonomic handles for garden tools

THE NATURAL GARDENING COMPANY
P.O. Box 750776
Petaluma, CA 94975-0776
707-766-9303
www.naturalgardening.com
Organic gardening supplies

OESCO, INC.
Route 116, P.O. Box 540
Conway, MA 01341
800-634-5557
www.oescoinc.com
Orchard equipment, supplies, hand tools

ORCHARD'S EDGE
836 Arlington Heights Road, No. 233
Elk Grove Village, IL 60007
877-881-1426
www.orchardsedge.com
Pruning equipment

THE ORIGINAL BUG SHIRT COMPANY
P.O. Box 127
Trout Creek, ON P0H 2L0
800-998-9096
www.bugshirt.com
Protective clothing

PARADISE WATER GARDENS
14 May Street
Whitman, MA 02382-1841
800-955-0161
www.paradisewatergardens.com
Water-garden supplies

PEACEFUL VALLEY FARM SUPPLY
P.O. Box 2209
Grass Valley, CA 95945
888-784-1722
www.groworganic.com
Organic supplies, tools, equipment

PLOW & HEARTH
P.O. Box 6000
Madison, VA 22727
800-494-7544
www.plowhearth.com
Garden furniture, accessories

RITTENHOUSE
Route 3, 1402 Fourth Avenue
St. Catharines, ON L2R 6P9
Canada
877-488-1914
www.rittenhouse.ca
Tools, equipment

SAMIA ROSE TOPIARY
1236 Urania Avenue
Encinitas, CA 92023
800-488-6742
www.srtopiary.com
Topiary frames, supplies

SMITH & HAWKEN
P.O. Box 431
Milwaukee, WI 53201
800-940-1170
www.smithandhawken.com
Hand tools, furniture, accessories

SNOW & NEALLEY
P.O. Box 876
Bangor, ME 04402
800-933-6642
www.snowandnealley.com
Tools

STILLBROOK HORTICULTURAL SUPPLIES
P.O. Box 600
Bantam, CT 06750
800-414-4468
www.stillbrook.com
Hand tools, trellises, accessories

WALT NICKE CO.
36 McLeod Lane
P.O. Box 433
Topsfield, MA 01983
800-822-4114
www.gardentalk.com
Tools, equipment, accessories

WATERFORD GARDENS
74 East Allendale Road
Saddle River, NJ 07458
201-327-0721
www.waterfordgardens.com
Water-garden supplies

WIND & WEATHER
1200 N. Main Street
Fort Bragg, CA 95437
800-922-9463
www.windandweather.com
Weather instruments, garden accessories

CONTRIBUTORS

JAKE CHAPLINE, a former editor for *Country Journal* and *Harrowsmith* magazines, can't grow many vegetables in the shady yard of his southern New Hampshire home but says that if he could eat slugs, he'd never have to go grocery shopping again. He has moved indoors for his latest writing project, a book on interior design.

KARAN DAVIS CUTLER, who has edited four previous BBG handbooks—*Salad Gardens, Tantalizing Tomatoes, Flowering Vines*, and *Starting From Seed*—gardens on 15 raccoon-infested acres in northern Vermont. A frequent contributor to several national garden magazines, her latest book is *The New England Gardener's Book of Lists* (2000).

CHERYL DORSCHNER is an award-winning columnist for the *Burlington Free Press* and a contributor to *Vermont Life* magazine. She gardens on two acres, where she maintains perennial beds and starts more than 100 different varieties of unusual annual flowers and vegetables from seed each year.

SYDNEY EDDISON, who has a passion for primroses and daylilies, has spent the last 40 years stuffing her Connecticut garden full of trees, shrubs, and perennials. She's especially interested in making "garden pictures"; her newest book, *The Gardener's Palette: Creating With Color* (2002), reflects this enthusiasm.

KATHLEEN FISHER, former editor of *The American Gardener,* maintains a perennial and herb garden in Alexandria, Virginia, and a frog pond in Reedville, Virginia. Her most recent books are *Herb Gardening for Dummies* (with Karan Davis Cutler, 2000), and *Taylor's Guide to Shrubs* (2001). She is also a contributor to the BBG handbook *Gourmet Herbs.*

BARRY GLICK is the owner of Sunshine Farm & Gardens, a nursery in West Virginia, and a prolific freelance writer. His articles have appeared in BBG's *Plants & Gardens News* and *Fine Gardening,* among other publications. He also writes a weekly plant column for his web site, www.sunfarm.com.

BARBARA PERRY LAWTON, garden editor of *St. Louis Homes & Life Styles,* wrote a weekly garden column for the *St. Louis Post-Dispatch* for 18 years. The author of *Magic of Irises* (1998) and the forthcoming *Mints, A Family of Herbs and Ornamentals,* and a contributor to the BBG handbook *Gourmet Herbs,* she lives and gardens on the banks of Missouri's Meramec River.

PETER LOEWER, who is also a movie reviewer, has written many books on gardening and natural history. His titles include *The Moonflower* (with Jean Loewer, 1998), an award-winning book for children. He gardens on one acre in western North Carolina, where he grows many of his plants from seed.

CHARLES W.G. SMITH is an environmental horticulturist and contributing editor of *Fine Gardening* magazine. He lives and gardens in the Berkshires of western Massachusetts, where he writes about gardening, nature, and outdoor recreation.

SALLY WILLIAMS, who gardens in Boston and Maine, is editor and publisher of *Garden Literature,* an index to periodical articles and book reviews. A compulsive reader and gardener, she is creating a garden on the site of a junkyard, a project that will last a lifetime.

ILLUSTRATIONS AND PHOTOS

EMMA SKURNICK illustrations
ALAN & LINDA DETRICK cover, pages 6, 26 right, 28, 36, 37, 42, 47, 59, 62, 69, 75, 77, 92, 96, 100
DEREK FELL pages 1, 4, 7, 14, 15, 21, 30, 33, 52, 60, 61, 64, 67, 74, 82
CHRISTINE DOUGLAS pages 9, 26 left, 44, 68, 90, 99
ELVIN McDONALD page 13
NEIL SODERSTROM pages 17, 18, 23, 24, 38, 41, 45, 46, 50, 54, 71, 78, 79, 93, 94
JERRY PAVIA pages 27, 39, 48, 63, 70, 72, 81, 95

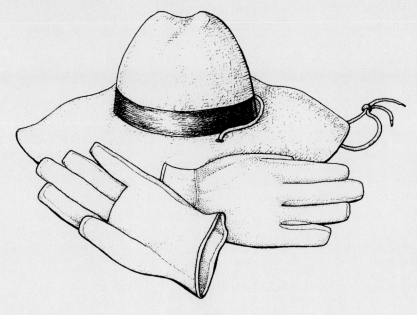

INDEX

BROOKLYN BOTANIC GARDEN

MICHAEL FUSCO

World renowned for pioneering gardening information, Brooklyn Botanic Garden's 21st-Century Gardening Series of award-winning guides provides spectacularly photographed, compact, practical advice for gardeners in every region of North America.

To order other fine titles published by BBG, call 718-623-7286, or shop in our online store at www.bbg.org/gardenemporium. For more information on Brooklyn Botanic Garden, including an online tour, visit www.bbg.org or call 718-623-7200.

MORE BOOKS ON GARDENING TOOLS AND TECHNIQUES

JOIN THE BROOKLYN BOTANIC GARDEN OR GIVE A GIFT OF MEMBERSHIP

Here are the membership benefits you can enjoy and share with others:

SUBSCRIBER $35

- Subscriptions to *21st-Century Gardening Series* handbooks and *Plants & Gardens News*
- Use of Gardener's Resource Center
- Reciprocal privileges at botanical gardens across the country

INDIVIDUAL $35

- One membership card for free individual admission
- 10% discount at the Garden Gift Shop
- Entry to members' summer hours, Sunset Picnics, and Preview Night at the Plant Sale
- Discounts on adult classes, trips, and tours
- *BBG Members News* and course catalog mailings
- Use of Gardener's Resource Center
- Reciprocal privileges at botanical gardens across the country

FAMILY/DUAL $65

All of the above INDIVIDUAL benefits, plus
- 2 membership cards for free admission for 2 adults & their children under 16
- Free parking for 4 visits
- 10% discount at the Terrace Cafe
- Discounts on children's programs and classes
- Subscriptions to *21st-Century Gardening Series* handbooks and *Plants & Gardens News*

FAMILY/DUAL PLUS $95

All of the above, plus
- 1 guest admitted free each time you come
- Free parking for 8 visits
- 2 SUBSCRIBER gift memberships for the price of one

SIGNATURE $150

All of the above, plus
- Your choice of one Signature Plant
- Free parking for 12 visits
- A special BBG gift calendar

SPONSOR $300

All of the above, plus
- Your choice of 2 Signature Plants
- 4 complimentary one-time guest passes
- Free parking for 18 visits

PATRON $500

All of the above, plus
- 2 guests admitted free each time you come
- Recognition in selected printed materials
- Free parking for 24 visits

GAGER SOCIETY $1500

All of the above, plus
- Unlimited free guests each time you come
- Gager Society Dinner and garden trip
- Complimentary INDIVIDUAL gift membership for a friend
- Private receptions for higher level donors
- Unlimited free parking for a year

Please use the form on reverse to join.
For more information, call the Membership Department: 718-623-7210

MEMBERSHIP FORM

Your Name

Address

City　　　　　　　　　**State**　　　　　**Zip**　　　**Membership#**

Daytime phone　　　　　　　　　**Evening phone**

email　　　　　　　　　　　　　❑ Check if this is a renewal.

Please enroll me as a member of the Brooklyn Botanic Garden.

❑ Subscriber $35　　　　❑ Signature $150
❑ Individual $35　　　　❑ Sponsor $300
❑ Family/Dual $65　　　❑ Patron $500
❑ Family/Dual Plus $95　❑ Gager Society $1500

Please send a gift membership to the recipient below.

❑ Subscriber $35　　　　❑ Signature $150
❑ Individual $35　　　　❑ Sponsor $300
❑ Family/Dual $65　　　❑ Patron $500
❑ Family/Dual Plus $95　❑ Gager Society $1500

Gift Recipient's Name

Address

City　　　　　　　　　**State**　　　　　**Zip**

Daytime phone　　　　　　　　　**Evening phone**

email

Method of Payment

❑ Check (payable to Brooklyn Botanic Garden)
❑ Visa ❑ MasterCard ❑ AMEX

Card #　　　　**Exp. Date**

Signature

Please tear along perforation, complete form and return with payment to:
Membership Office, Brooklyn Botanic Garden,
1000 Washington Avenue, Brooklyn, NY 11225-1099
Phone: 718-623-7210 Fax: 718-857-2430